The Destroying Angel

A Tale of Love

Shirley Turner

Published by Piscataqua Press
142 Fleet St. Portsmouth, NH 03801
www.ppressbooks.com

Printed in the United States

ISBN: 978-1-944393-63-2

The Destroying Angel

for my son, William

My life has been a story of wandering,
and I mark the events in my life
by the places I have lived.

An Historical Introduction to
The Destroying Angel

Advised by several literary agents and editors that her manuscript was compelling and rife with commercial potential but needed the skills of a professional co-writer to make it publishable, Shirley Turner contacted the English Department at the University of Maine. Her request for help included some of the details in this memoir, and perhaps because I have long taught Richard Hoffman's *Half the House*, I was drawn to her story.

I contacted Shirley and soon discovered a woman of conviction and honesty who battles the devastating effects of long term physical, mental, and sexual abuse of the most vile kind, with a resilience and courage I have never before encountered.

I knew in short order that my part in bringing this memoir to print would be to locate a female writer with both the compassion and courage to shape this story without compromising it in any way, and not as a co-writer myself. This is a memoir that requires no comment or analysis. It needed only a gentle and loving polish.

Over the course of two years, three women took up and then abandoned the cause due to the intensity of Shirley's manuscript, before I met Tina Passman, the Angel who shepherded this book into its present narrative form. She tinkered with little but syntax, grammar, and punctuation, with an eye to eliminating repeated information. By faithfully preserving Shirley's voice, Tina allows this story to unfold as if the reader were hearing it over coffee at Shirley and Paul's house on a snowy Maine afternoon. Nothing has been held back, but neither has anything been accentuated for effect. This is the straightforward telling of as difficult a story as I have ever heard.

In the end, this is a journey of triumph, a story that exalts the incredible courage of one human being who refused to buckle under a barrage of despair, hatred, and trauma, inspired by the one pure love of her life.

Bruce Pratt

Chapter 1
Meadville, Pennsylvania

I was born in 1962 in Meadville, Pennsylvania.

When I was born, my father was having an affair at the same time that he was married to my mother. When I was two, my parents' marriage ended. I ended up being tossed from my grandparents' house to my aunt's house, then back to my mom's house. I remember many older men hanging around our house; my mother didn't have any permanent man in her life.

I loved the stability of life with my grandparents. Although my life was very confusing for me, I had a lot of fun with them. They took me to Conneaut Lake Park many times; we often went to a place that made homemade custard in a little cup. Was it ever delicious!

I know that my grandparents loved me very much. My grandmother bathed me and kept me clean and fed me the very best of the food at her house. My grandfather took me to the bank every Saturday to get me a silver dollar for my jar; he had been collecting silver dollars for me to have someday when I grew up.

(That was when they were made of real silver.)

When I went to stay at my aunt and uncle's house, I was very well taken care of. My aunt and uncle had two children and were making ends meet. I remember going there once and my aunt took out 6 or 8 boxes of cereal She said to me, "Have what ever one you want, Shirley." I had never known anyone to have that many different kinds of cereal before! It just stuck in my head like a dream I had.

After awhile, I went back to live with my mother. There was not anything to spare when it came to money. I ate an awful lot of potpies at the time! I got a new stepfather soon after that, who, in later years, committed suicide with a gun. I don't remember much about him, only that he was a kind and caring man.

It wasn't long before I was back at my grandparents' and aunt's houses again. I missed my mom a lot. I remember my uncle telling me that my mother didn't care about me or she would be taking care of me, instead of out running around. My grandmother spoke up, saying, "Don't tell her that - she'll remember that." And, of course, I did.

I played Barbies at my aunt and uncle's house with my cousins. My grandfather read me stories. One of my fondest memories was riding my little green tricycle around and around the dining room table. I rode all over the house, bumping into my grandparents' furniture. I know I must have done some damage, but they never said a word to me. I also remember going up to my playroom to play with my teddy bear and tea set.

My uncle lived with my grandparents. He never married nor had any children. He had several girl friends but nothing ever came of it. I have often wondered why, especially in light of events in the family, which I will recount in this narrative. On several occasions when I was upstairs playing with my tea set and toys, my uncle screamed at me to quiet down, saying that I was making too much noise. He was working a nighttime job at the time and I was disturbing his sleep. He worked as a truck driver for a mushroom company in Pennsylvania.

When I upset my uncle, my grandmother would take me downstairs to play. One day, I was running around the house and tripped on a cord that was stretched across the floor and split my chin right open. They took me to the doctor but there wasn't much that he could do except stitch it up and call it good enough.

I enjoyed outings as well. My grandfather took me for walks to the nearby college to show me off to the college students. He would sit there for hours at a time and brag about me. Maybe he was helping the college students to decide whether they wanted children! He also walked me all the way to downtown Meadville to buy things especially for me. He would buy sausage straight from the butcher to give to my grandmother, so she could cook me sausage and pancakes. My favorite breakfast! He would buy little toys for me to play with. I was his favorite grandchild, and he told this to everyone around him. I am so glad that someone thought I was really special!

We used to go across the river to Little Cooley in Pennsylvania to visit some of my grandparents' friends, who had a very nice house. My grandfather and uncle also took me fishing on several occasions. I remember catching a sunfish - I was so proud of myself, and I think my grandfather was as well. Once, I even went out on my uncle's boat.

I truly had a wonderful life at that time. My life was all right because everyone else in my life made up for the lack of my mother being there. I wish I could have had her love and attention, but that isn't the way it was. She was out looking for another man.

Chapter 2
Carmel & Hallowell, Maine

My mother found a man and I wish she never had found this particular man. She met him at the Meadville, Pennsylvania State Fair. I was crying at the time for a soda, and he bought me one. I wonder if he was trying to impress my mom. I know she went off with him that night and I was left at my grandparents' house.

We moved to Carmel, Maine.

That year, at Christmas time I stood in front of an old floor model TV where you had to change channels manually. I had on my black velvet dress with the white lace, holding my new Teddy bear, given to me by my new stepfather.

After a while, my mother became pregnant with my sister. When she was about 8 or 9 months pregnant, my new father began molesting me. He took me down to the spring in Carmel. He made the excuse that he was taking me to pick flowers, which I truly loved long

5

before I ever met him. He abused me mentally and sexually. My stepfather had oral sex with me regularly and masturbated. I closed my eyes and hoped and prayed it would be over. To this day, every time I drive by the Ash Hill road in Carmel, I have anxiety attacks from the traumas I experienced from my stepfather's sexual abuse. I was 5 years old.

Although we are taught we are not supposed to hate, I hated him! He never considered what it he was doing to me. I certainly wasn't supposed to be having sexual experiences at 5 years old. This was the mental and physical abuse of a child.

We lived at his mother's house. I awoke my sister from a nap one day and my stepfather's mother punished me by locking me in the chicken coop all day in the hot sun with no food or water.

My stepfather was growing Panama Red marijuana in his mother's tomato plants, until the day she said that they were going to have company, and that he had to pull the plants. He whined that he couldn't let them grow long enough to get the seeds. He brought the seeds with him back from Panama after serving his country in the Vietnam War. He had brought home two ounces with him, and hoped to cultivate more.

We were constantly moving, but never strayed far away from his mother and father in Maine for any length of time. My mother's family was in

Pennsylvania, and I hardly ever got to see them. I believe he was keeping us away from them so that he could abuse us and they would not know it.

We lived in Hallowell, Maine for a while in a basement apartment. One day, I refused to clean my room. My stepfather got me up in the middle of the night to clean it. He screamed and raved at me until it was done. My sister was a little baby, and he was yelling so much that he woke her up. I finally did get it done. I had to go to school the next day. I was so tired! But I never let my room get messy again.

Even my mother was abusive to me. One time she was rocking my sister in the rocking chair and I was sitting on the floor next to her. She rocked on my fingers; she didn't say anything to me but, "You shouldn't of had your fingers under there." She didn't stop rocking my sister to see if I was all right. I went to my bed and cried for a while.

We had to keep moving because he spent all his money on drugs, so he never paid the rent. My mother's husband was constantly fighting with someone. It could be anyone, anywhere, at any time. It was like living with a time bomb and you never knew when or what would set it off. Once we were in the car, driving down the road, and he had my mother crushing up a bud of marijuana and she dropped it on the floor. That was, of course, the last of it. My stepfather beat

7

my mom so badly that she had a seizure and I didn't know if she was going to come out of it. He told us that he was going to drive down this dead end road and murder us all. My sister and I started crying, she in her car seat and I in my seat belt.

I only remember one time that we went out to eat at McDonald's, when the first one opened in Rockland, Maine.

Chapter 3
Rockland, Maine

We moved to a big house in Rockland. I was 8 or 10 years old. It was an old sea captain's house by the ocean and I had a yard to play in at last! My sister and I were so excited just to go out in our own yard.

My stepfather was breaking into people's houses to support his drug problem. He even went so far as to steal someone's Christmas presents from under their Christmas tree to give to us on Christmas. I would have rather not had any gifts at all, seeing that they were stolen. Talk about the Grinch stealing Christmas - it really happened to us! He even stole people's coin collections that he heard about through his drug buddies. He bragged about doing it.

He hooked up with this one guy and they went into a woman's house the first thing in the morning. They had packed a lunch and stayed there the entire day until it was dark again and safe to leave. It took them the entire day to find the coin collection - the little old lady had it hidden in a linen closet in the bathroom along with her silver service. I thought that was a pretty smart woman. He threw the silver away in a quarry in Rockland, because it could have been identified. The silver set was probably in their family for generations, getting passed down each generation. I feel so bad for these people; it hurts me to know this information.

He stored the coins in an old piano that we had in the house because he figured that if we got raided the police wouldn't look in there. One day, I went over to the piano and tried to play it. It made a funny noise and my mother told me that the coins were in there and to get away from it.

There was a big barn in the sea captain's house and my stepfather would have drug parties and glue sniffing parties and pill parties, even doing cocaine and shooting up. I walked in on the parties many times.

My stepfather had sex with me up there in the barn or even in the house. I also found out that his brother was having sex with his girlfriend's daughter. His girlfriend stood up to him. My stepfather's brother beat the daylights out of her for confronting him about it at our house in front of everyone. But I personally was so glad that the girl's mother had enough nerve to stand up to him. It was too bad he beat her, and they broke up shortly after that. I was glad for the girl to get away from the abuse, unlike me. Besides my mom and me, my stepfather was having sex with other people.

Years later, he and I were hitch hiking and a van stopped. The people in it beat him severely. I think he had either molested or swindled them.

I was constantly teased and pushed down at school. I was chased home. Other children shoved me off the swings and the merry go round. They even threw rocks at me as I ran home. I think this was because I was so different. When I fell down, they'd hover over me and call me names. It was like I had a target on my forehead. I'd go home with my knees all skinned up and my mom would bandage them up for me. I never went to the principal's office or anything like that. I never made trouble. That would embarrass her.

My stepfather was consumed with drugs. I know my mother was doing them sometimes as well. But she couldn't do drugs all the time because she had her children under her feet. She had chores to do to keep the house running. She had to please my stepfather. My mother cooked and kept the house just spotless. But she never spent much quality time with me. She did teach me to keep the house clean, and I remember scrubbing the mopboards on my hands and knees.

She had an old wringer washer for the longest time, which took a great deal of time and energy. Somehow my stepfather came into some money and she got a real washer - wasn't she thrilled with that! I will never forget that day! She danced around the kitchen like she was a teenager.

The Destroying Angel

In 1974, my grandparents came to visit us in Rockland. I will never forget my grandfather reading to me, going out in the yard and playing ball with my sister and me. We went to Cascade Park in Bangor. We scraped the pitch off a spruce gum tree and chewed it.

My grandfather bought me a brand new bicycle - my stepfather wasn't happy about it - but I was thrilled. At that time, bell-bottom pants were in style, and I got them caught in my bike chain. This nice old couple stopped to cut my pants loose so I could ride home. My parents weren't happy about my pants, but I like to think they were glad I made it home okay.

My grandparents were so good to me - how I missed them! I wish they could have stayed forever. Maybe the sexual abuse would have stopped. Or maybe I could have gone home with them. To this day, I wonder how my life would have been. I know that my parents were on welfare. I guess they needed me for the check.

One day my stepfather brought home a chicken that flew off the back of a truck on the way to the slaughterhouse. He chased it back and forth through a fence until it finally got so tired it just sat there and gave up. it had lost so many feathers it was almost bald. My mother and stepfather put it in the cellar and fed it regularly. It perched on the furnace at night - you should have seen the furnace man's face when he had to repair it one day and found that chicken poop all over it! My mother opened the basement door one day and said to my stepfather, "Look what that stupid rooster did." There was an egg on the top step of the cellar stairs! My stepfather said. "That's no rooster - I got a hen." We had plenty of eggs after that for a long time.

My stepfather never had any remorse for his crimes, and probably doesn't to this day.

Chapter 4
Rockland, Maine

We ended up selling our house and moving to an apartment in the same town, Rockland, Maine. It was a small place compared to the big house and yard we left. My sister and I had to share a room together, and that was a wonderful thing for me. I was able to get to know her more. She wasn't under mom's wing. We shared many good times together. We had gotten "Light Brights" the previous Christmas and played with them so much we had to get new papers to make the pictures. We made cabins under our school desks with blankets.

My stepfather had gotten the desks at the town dump.

He would sell items he got at the dump in an ongoing yard sale out on the front lawn. He put some of the stolen items into the yard sale to get rid of the evidence and make a profit. He ended up getting hepatitis from the dump and brought it home to my mom. They were very sick.

My stepfather's mother came down to help around the house until they got better from the hepatitis. That was the only time he didn't creep into my bedroom and sexually abuse me, because she shared my bed with me one night and my sister's bed the next night. She said that sleeping with me was like sleeping with a mule - that I kicked all night long. Maybe it was because her son was abusing me. I was having nightmares.

Even though I was sharing my bedroom with his blood daughter, he would still come into our room at night and molest me. In the middle of the night he told my mother he couldn't sleep and needed to get a buzz to get back to sleep. He would smoke a joint then come in to molest me. Our bedroom was directly across from their bedroom. She was ignoring what he was doing to me or afraid he would hurt her if she said anything about it. I felt so dirty after he would do this to me, especially since my sister was in an adjacent bed in the same room. I knew she looked up to me. I did what I was forced to do. He threatened to murder me, my mom, and my sister - and then himself - if I didn't do what he wanted. I believed him.

My stepfather was and still is crazy. At that time, he was doing things like drinking wine with prescription drugs that people would bring him, selling marijuana and smoking it, shooting crystal meth into his veins. So I knew he was crazy and that he would do anything to get high. That is why I believed he would have killed us, if I didn't do what he wanted.

He constantly had people coming into our home to buy or sell drugs. Often they would bring stolen items to swap for drugs. My mother constantly complained to my stepfather about all of the traffic that was making a mess on her kitchen floor. My mother did teach me to embroider a little sampler she got in a kit for me. I was so happy that she thought of me and spent time with me to show me how to do it! It was a wonderful experience for me. Years later she still had the sampler and gave it to me. I will always treasure that. I put it in a picture frame and hung it on my wall to look at every day, to remind me of the experience and time she spent with me. For that period of time, I had a mother.

There was a gentleman that lived down stairs in a room that he rented from the landlord. He asked me to come into his room one day. I was very frightened, but he left the door open so I knew I could run out if I needed to. He had a complete set of sterling silver flatware that had been in his family for years and he didn't have any child to give it to, so he decided to sell it and asked me if it was worth anything. I was just a kid, but he saw me out there tending the yard sale a lot and asked me. I replied that our items were all priced and that if I didn't know I asked my parents. He said, "well tell them about this and see if they will come down and see it." That's what I did.

My stepfather offered him 20 dollars for all of it. He was really happy to get that amount, but my stepfather got more than that, of course, when he sold it. He actually ripped this little old man off. My stepfather said to my mother that the old man would go out and buy himself a bottle and he would be as happy as a clam. So my mom must have been questioning him about how much he had given him for the silverware, and she must have felt a little guilty even though she didn't make the deal.

My stepfather had some houseplants in the living room, which he fed fishmeal juice from the fish plant across the street. One evening, I was watching television; I wasn't really paying much attention while eating my popcorn. I dropped a piece of popcorn under my chair. I picked it up and tossed it into my mouth. It didn't turn out to popcorn at all. It was a mud ball that I tossed right into my mouth. What an awful taste of fishmeal juice it was!

My grandparents came to visit us and we went to Camden, into some gift shops, down to Searsport, to the flea markets and more gift shops. We had a really good time.

The Destroying Angel

I told my grandparents what my stepfather was doing to me at night. My grandfather never said anything, but my grandmother replied, "He's too good of a man - he couldn't be doing such a thing." Why didn't she believe me? It was so heartbreaking for me.

The landlord downstairs was an alcoholic and his son was into everything illegal, even dealing stolen guns. They fought a lot. My stepfather went down one day and confronted the son about beating on his father. That's when the war broke out between them and us. They wanted us to move out of there then. My parents stopped paying rent, and my parents took shifts watching the place; of course, my mother had days and my stepfather had nights, which gave him complete access to me.

We scarcely dared to leave. Mom took us in a cab when she went to get groceries and such because she didn't have a driver's license. My stepfather took the car when he wanted to go out. It got to the point where the landlord and his son were out in the yard threatening to shoot out our kitchen windows with a shotgun. Then they shot out the windows in his Cadillac, parked in the yard. My parents decided to send my sister and me to his mother's house in Bangor. They told us we would be safe there. I was worried I would never see my mother again.

My stepfather's mother taught me to crochet to

18

pass the time away and to keep my mind off of missing my mother. We did get to see our parents in a week or so, but it was the first time we had been away from our parents in a very long time. My parents decided to move out of state then.

Chapter 5
Connecticut

We stopped in to visit my grandparents and it was the last time I would ever see them. I had a really good time there and my stepfather didn't abuse me, either. Then, he decided we would live in Connecticut, where my stepfather's cousin lived. His cousin had a cottage on the river, and my stepfather and mother made a plan to rent it for a while. My stepfather got a job in a print shop making good money. My mother stayed home.

I had a room that was actually a hallway next to the bathroom. My stepfather slept on the couch in the living room. And my mother slept with my sister in the master bedroom. His excuse to come into my room was to use the bathroom. He claimed he slept on the couch because he had to get up so many times in the night and he didn't want to wake everyone up. Wasn't my mother a little suspicious that he wasn't sleeping in her bed and my sister was?

An Indian brother and sister lived across the road. They were very nice. I had never known a pure blooded Indian before, and it was quite a learning experience for me. The sister made the most beautiful beadwork that I had ever seen. She sold the items she made at pow wows and other events that they attended. Her brother used to shoot a bow and arrow at a target out in the yard. I don't think he ever missed. Her house always smelled like bread baking or cookies. I loved to go over there to visit!

I wish we could have lived in Connecticut longer. While we were there we did get to go to a pow wow, invited by our friends. We all had so much fun and saw authentic dances performed right before us! It was an exciting and important time in my life. My great grandmother was a full-blooded Indian herself and my great grandfather was white, and an alcoholic. They had thirteen children together. My great grandmother became ill and couldn't take care of the children. My great grandfather beat her so badly trying to get her up to take care of all of the children that she died. The children were divided up amongst the neighborhood. The only child I got to know was my grandmother, and she was a toddler at the time when this all happened. I think it traumatized her for life. It was certainly a tragedy for our family.

While we lived in Connecticut, I went to a Salvation

The Destroying Angel

Army camp for an entire week, which meant no sexual abuse for a week. It was absolutely wonderful! I learned how to weave a basket and I tried to learn to swim, but there were so many other kids there that I wasn't able to get the attention I needed to learn. I had a good time, and at the same time missed my mother and sister.

Sometimes my mother took peanut butter and spread it on the tree outside of the dining room window. The chickadees would have a good time with it. The peanut butter would get all over their beaks and they would sit there and scrape it off for the longest time before they finally flew off.

One morning, my mother asked me to wash some dishes and I missed some food on one of the plates. My mother had me wash those dishes all that day over and over again. When my stepfather got home from work that night, he asked me what I was doing. I told him. He beat my mother so badly she had a seizure. Another time, I started chewing my fingernails, and my mother's solution to the problem was that every time I washed my hands I was supposed to put my fingers in hot sauce. Then, when I'd put my fingernails into my mouth to bite my nails, my mouth would burn.

At the time, I didn't know what to think. It almost seemed like my mother knew my stepfather was molesting me and she hated me for it, when I was the victim. At the same time, she was a victim, being abused by him herself.

We had some mallard ducks and they had their own little swimming pool. My stepfather threw lettuce in there, and they loved that and grasshoppers he would catch. They had their wings clipped so they couldn't fly away.

My mother took a part time job taking care of an elderly man that lived down the street, who couldn't do much for himself at all. But he had a lot of prescription pain killer drugs lying around. My stepfather talked my mother into stealing them for him. Then he contacted this guy from Rockland that he knew and he sold them to him for money and marijuana.

Chapter 6
Bangor, Maine

Shortly after that, we moved from Connecticut to Bangor, Maine. At first we lived with my stepfather's mother. For a few weeks, until we could get our own place, it was pretty hectic. My mother and his mother didn't like each other. They put on airs like they did, but at times it would just show. There was one good thing about living at her house. I didn't get sexually molested there.

I remember that his mother would duct tape my mouth shut when we were in the car because she said she couldn't concentrate on her driving, saying that I talked too much. But maybe I was just excited to go for a ride. My grandfather never complained about my talking and he drove me to a lot of places when I was living with them.

When we finally moved into our own place, it was right down the street from my stepfather's mother's house. She was there quite a bit.

Shirley Turner

I was thirteen when my stepfather took the sexual abuse to the next level. He forced me to do oral sex on him. He said if I didn't do what he wanted he would murder us all, then kill himself, so I did what I was told. I had to go to school with herpes on my mouth. It was very embarrassing to me. At the time, I didn't know what it was or where I had gotten it. He also started showing me pictures of kids and women in magazines and asked me if I would do the things they were doing in them. I said no, I didn't want to. He wanted me to pose nude for him so he could send pictures of me to the magazines. I refused, telling him I was doing what he wanted already, and that I shouldn't have to do that, too.

A few weeks went by and I was up in my room. He forced me again. My mother crept up the stairs and opened the door, and demanded to know how long this had been going on! Oh my gosh! I thought my nightmare was finally going to end!

I went down stairs, and she asked me again, how long this had been going on. I explained to her that he had been molesting me since I was 5 years old. She told me that it would ease up on her a little now. I said to myself, "She doesn't really care about me." I didn't know what to do. If I didn't do what my stepfather wanted, he would threaten to kill my mother and sister. My life was still the same terrible life.

The Destroying Angel

My sister fell down out in the yard and developed an abscess on her knee. She was laid up on the couch for a week or more. When she couldn't walk any more, my stepfather finally opened it up and cleaned all of the puss out of it. Her knee got better, and after a week she was back to school again.

There was a boy at school that really liked me, and one day he walked me home and kissed me. My stepfather was watching from inside and was not pleased about this. That's when he raped me for the first time. I was only 13 years old. It hurt me so much that I cried and cried. Of course, he wouldn't let me go to any school dances or anything that would bring me into contact with boys. I was to come home directly from school and that was it.

Chapter 7
Bangor, Maine

This time to another school in another district.

I never got to see that boy again. And that's what my stepfather wanted. Our next apartment was the lower part of an entire house but it was rather small. We did, however, stay in the Bangor, Maine area.

My sister and I had to sleep in the same bed. Don't you think that he would have stopped molesting me where I was sleeping in the same bed with his own daughter? Later in life, my sister told me that she saw him have sex with me, and rolled over on her side and prayed that he would not come after her. He went back to bed afterward.

My stepfather often beat my mother and afterwards she would have a seizure. She slept for hours after the seizures. Once she had one and it was so bad that she chewed her tongue so badly that it was just like hamburger. She had to drink from a straw and take tiny little sips of broth.

The Destroying Angel

My stepfather was dealing drugs to minors in our house. We had many strange people coming and going all the time, day or night. I tried not bathing for an entire week, to discourage him from having sex with me. But he went to my mother and told her that I hadn't had a bath in a long time, so she put me in an ice cold shower with my clothes on. She said that I couldn't come out until I was clean. I don't understand why she didn't ask me why I didn't want to take a shower; she really knew why. I have already described how at our last residence she walked into the room while my stepfather was forcing me to have oral sex with him. Why didn't she go to the police or do anything? This question has haunted me my entire life.

I had a school report to do, and the teacher said for extra credit I could dress the part. My cousin had sent me some of her old clothes, all the way from Florida. And there happened to be the perfect dress in the box. It looked like a pilgrim dress. My report was on the trading the Indians and Pilgrims did when the Pilgrims came to America. The dress had a string that crisscrossed in the front of the dress. I tried it on the night before and my stepfather tore it off me, instead of loosening the strings. I asked my mother if she could sew it in time for school the following day. She refused, and pinned it. I looked awful, and I was embarrassed at school. I did get a good grade, however.

That's when my stepfather began giving me marijuana to control me further.

A family bought the house across the street from us, and I got to know the young girl that lived there. She had a brother that was younger than her. The girl came right out and told me that her stepfather was molesting her. So I thought it was a normal that stepfathers were sexual with their stepchildren. In another way it was very painful to me. We didn't live there much longer - my mother had a good relationship with the girl's mother and I really enjoyed talking with the girl. My stepfather couldn't stand that, that we both had a friend. Only his mother could be our friend.

Chapter 8

Jacksonville, Florida and Lewiston, Maine

We moved to Jacksonville, Florida. We sold everything we had again, including a stolen Panasonic TV. My stepfather got an old 1964 or '65 Fleetwood Cadillac. He had to put a new motor in it, which he got from the junkyard. We used a case and a half of oil on the way down to Florida! When we got there, we didn't have any money left. We ended up living in a housing complex in Jacksonville. Some people might call it "the 'hood." We all slept on the floor - we had no furniture. My mother borrowed some dishes and pots and pans from a neighbor.

One day, I came home from school and my stepfather was beating my mother. She went into a seizure. At that point, he kidnapped my sister and me and headed for the highway, which was close to the housing complex. I feared that he might have seriously injured her, and left her for dead.

We ended up hitchhiking from Florida to Maine. My

stepfather didn't have much money, and we were hungry. He stopped at a Howard Johnson Restaurant, but the only thing on the menu we had enough money for was a half an English muffin each and a glass of milk. The lady at another table was complaining that her English muffin was burnt. My stepfather spoke up and said, "If you're going to throw that out, I have two little girls here that are hungry that I'm sure would eat it." The waitress looked at the woman and then at us, and said, "Certainly." When we were about to leave, an older couple said to my stepfather, "Can we give you a lift wherever you're going?" We were going to Maine and they were going to Providence, Rhode Island.

They took us as far as they could. Along the way the man had a flat tire on a bridge, so my stepfather got out and changed the tire for the man. The traffic was rushing by them. The couple continued on until their turnoff to Rhode Island, and the lady reached into her pocket book and gave my stepfather $50. She said to him, "Get these girls off of the highway before something bad happens to them." So he went into the closest town and bought us all a ticket to Portland, Maine. When we arrived, my stepfather called his mother collect and asked her to come and get us. She was a little reluctant, it was such a long way for her to drive, but she came. She took us to her house for a while.

The Destroying Angel

My stepfather got a job down in Lewiston, Maine, and we moved into an apartment, using money that he had borrowed from his mother. He let me attend two weeks of high school, until the day he asked me if the boys were looking at me and I replied yes, they always do. That was my last day of school. My sister, however, got to continue her schooling and I was happy she could.

My stepfather was away during the day and I had the house to clean. I also took care of my sister. I helped her with her homework after school. My stepfather was molesting me at night after my sister went to sleep. I worried about whether I would ever see my mother again. I wondered if this nightmare would end. My sister cried a lot, and told my stepfather that she missed her mom and that I did, too. I wondered if my mother had even survived the attack and the seizure she had suffered from his beating and his abandonment of her.

Chapter 9
Jacksonville, Florida

I couldn't believe my eyes - one day I opened the door, and my mother was there! I thought the nightmare was finally over. My sister and I had our first plane flight back to Jacksonville, Florida. Oh, the next 3 months were wonderful! But my mother still had contact with my stepfather's mother. My stepfather had gotten a job in a college as an offset pressman. He was living with his mother in her housing complex.

He ended up taking a bus down to Jacksonville, got a job, and started supporting our family. He slept on the couch again right outside of my bedroom. My mother and sister slept in the bedroom in the full sized bed. Why did my mother want him to come back again? There was no sexual contact between them.

An elderly gentleman had moved into the apartment downstairs. My mother was baking and cooking for this man. He had money, and I guess her plan was to move in with this man, because he bought a piece of land and a trailer and they all ended up living happily together.

I found this out 15 years later when I went to see them. Why didn't my mother keep me and give me a better life, as she did for my sister? Not that I am jealous of my sister; I am glad she was able to have a better life. She was able to go to college and have a somewhat normal life. I still don't understand why my mother didn't care enough about me to keep me as well. The only thing I can figure is that she thought I was stealing her man and she hated me for that. I was so happy when my stepfather wasn't in my life. It was absolutely wonderful! But, he was back, and so was the nightmare.

I was almost 15 years old, and my stepfather asked me to ask my friend at school if she could get some marijuana. A few days later she brought me some. A few more days passed, and I asked her if her stepfather molested her. She said, "No, he would never do anything like that." By now, I was really wondering what was going to happen to me.

In about a week, the department of human services was at our door. They asked me what my stepfather was doing to me. I told them the truth, that he was having sex with me. So they shackled and chained my stepfather right then and there, and put him in jail. My stepfather wrote letters to my mother, begging her to get him out of there. My mother forced me to go to the police station and tell them it was a lie, when it certainly wasn't a lie.

Why didn't she tell the police he was doing this, and protect me from him? I think she hated the truth and it was easier just to blame me, when I was the victim.

When my stepfather got out of jail, he and my mother argued. My mother said to my stepfather, "Take her and get out of my house! All you did was screw up my welfare check coming back here!" But at least this time he didn't beat my mother.

My stepfather made me pack a backpack with a few pieces of clothing and took me on the road hitchhiking.

Chapter 10
On the road

My stepfather kept me from my family for 15 years, telling me that they didn't want me. After many years, I was really beginning to wonder if he wasn't right. I would have protected my daughter instead of throwing her away to her abuser. I know my mother had mental problems and trouble dealing with life in general. But I was her flesh and blood, and blood is supposed to be thicker than water. You just don't give your child away to anyone, no matter what!

He took me and got out of her house. My stepfather took me to the interstate and hitch-hiked to Maine. A trucker stopped to pick us up. He was taking some kind of speed, offered it to my stepfather, but he didn't take any. Every time the driver shifted the truck into gear, he slid his hand underneath my bottom. I would move over a little and when my stepfather finally asked me why I kept moving over, I whispered in his ear what the truck driver was doing to me. My stepfather asked the truck driver to let us out immediately. It was dark, the middle of the night, and the trucker dropped us off right in the middle of the Bronx.

There are good truckers out there and we rode with many others that were perfect gentleman.

A policeman saw us, stopped, and asked, "What are you doing here at this time of night?" He said, "Get out of here!" My stepfather replied, "I don't have any money. We are from Maine and don't know what to do." The policeman found a cab driver right in the area, and told him to get us out of there. The cab driver did, and that policeman probably saved my life. My stepfather got a motel room with the last of his money. The following day he called his mother collect and asked her to Western Union some money so we could make it to Maine. We hitchhiked the rest of the way. This was in 1977.

Chapter 11
Lewiston, Maine

For the 1st two weeks we slept in a cabin the kids from the neighborhood had made in Lewiston, Maine. They would come and visit us and get high on marijuana there. We slept on old car seats at night and during the day we would look for jobs. My stepfather finally asked his mother for some money to rent an apartment.

He also knew this woman whom he had been engaged to in high school, many years earlier, and he had backed out of marrying her. We often went to her mother's house and do laundry and clean out her garage for her. For payment, she fed us meals while we were there. When it came to paying us money for the job we had done, she would only pay my stepfather, because I did my laundry there. She even gave us pots and pans to start life in a new apartment; I still have some of those very same pots and pans. I never understood why these people never called child protective services to report my stepfather for the crime he was committing. But it was over 30 years ago.

Once or twice we ended up seeing the woman he was supposed to marry, and it was a very difficult situation. I wish my stepfather had married her. She was a really nice lady, and I might have had a different life. But you can't cry over the past, you can only move forward and change your future.

My stepfather and I both got jobs in the same week. I began working at a shoe shop. I was only 15 years old, but my stepfather told me to tell them I was 18 years old. I believe the Social Security Agency finally contacted the shoe shop, because after a few months the people started harassing me to make me quit my job.

My stepfather worked at a print shop. We didn't have money for food, so we went to the Salvation Army. They gave us an in-store credit of five dollars. We bought a box of tea bags, a bag of sugar, a gallon of milk, and some macaroni and cheese. When we ran out of food, I climbed into the dumpster behind Dunkin Donuts and got their day old donuts. They were all clean and in a separate bag from the garbage. We ate them for about 2 weeks, until we got our first checks.

At work a lady asked me why I ate Dunkin Donuts everyday for lunch. I replied that was all I had to eat. She just walked away. After a few days passed, my stepfather told me to ask my boss for an advance on my pay until I got my check. He said no, so we continued to eat donuts. To this day it is hard for me to eat a Dunkin Donut!

We were also picking marijuana roaches in the park underneath the benches.

When we got our first checks we paid the rent, bought food, and he bought a bag of marijuana. He still had me under control and he was always telling me that no one wanted me, isolating me from my family.

One night, I awoke, seeing the reflection of a fire on our window. I woke my stepfather, and he told me to get dressed and get out of there. We found out the house across the street was on fire. It and three others that burned to the ground that night. It was such a sad thing that happened - two people lost their lives, and about a hundred people were homeless, all in the same night. I think it frightened my stepfather that we were living on the fourth floor, because it wasn't long afterwards that we moved again.

Chapter 12
Lewiston, Maine

We moved to another house in Lewiston, and lived on the second floor. When we decided to move out, I asked the landlady if we could get a reference from her to rent another apartment. Her reply was, "You give $20.00 and I give you a good reference." That's just how she put it, when I had left the place so nice and clean.

My mother and father called me and asked me to come back to Florida. But I refused. I knew my mother didn't really want me or she wouldn't have done what she did by throwing me away to my stepfather. I didn't really know my father. He hadn't ever been in my life. My stepfather had told me over and over that if they ever came after me to remember they threw me away. So I took all of this into consideration and said no. Of course, all my stepfather was doing was thinking of himself. He told me things like, "If I didn't do those things to you, I wouldn't have you today." But he wasn't supposed to have me. He would have gotten someone else, and he would have lost me. He never considered how it would affect me as an adult. It certainly has affected me in so many ways. I lived through years of mental, physical, and sexual abuse. The pain and suffering he put me through has given me an illness called Post Traumatic Stress Disorder. Because this man traumatized me in every way possible, and for so long, I have a lot of anxiety, depression, and concentration problems. I also have a number of other health concerns.

My stepfather told me to call my grandfather and ask for my silver dollars; when my grandfather asked my uncle, he replied no. To this day, I'm glad he did. My husband would have sold them for drugs, and my grandfather wanted me to save them for college or something very special just for me.

I found out years later that my grandfather asked my uncle to go out and shovel the walkway, and my uncle refused. My grandfather was a very proud man, and if someone wouldn't do it for him, he would do it himself, and that's what he did. After he was done, he came into the house and collapsed in his chair. He had a heart attack and died.

Chapter 13

St. Albans, Maine
Darlington, South Carolina

We moved to St Albans, Maine. We stayed at a place that my stepfather's brother had stayed there before, and slept in an old Cadillac hearse for a while. We hitch-hiked to the local store. It was about 4 or 5 miles one way. We used to travel that distance to the local store for food. We hitch hiked into Bangor almost every weekend to take a bath at his mother's house. We got food stamps.

After a while, my stepfather borrowed enough money to get us on our way to try and find jobs down South for the winter months. We didn't have enough money to rent an apartment. As I think about it now, I realize he was on the run with me. I did what I was told to do, and that hoped one day I would make it through this nightmare. I wanted to see my family again.

We were on our way to Darlington, South Carolina, to work for my stepfather's mother's cousin. We cleaned cars for two weeks waiting for payment, and when it was time to get paid, the cousin said I didn't work as hard as my stepfather did, so he wasn't going to pay me. I'm sure it was because I was under age and he could get away with it.

We ended up staying with one of the workers for a few weeks, and then he kicked us out. The people behind his trailer were Mormons from Utah, who were studying in Darlington and trying to establish a church there. They told us about some nice people across town that took in people sometimes. We lived there for 2 or 3 weeks. It was a very different way of life. I had never eaten goat meat, and one day they decided to kill a pig out in the yard. They asked some men to come over to do this in exchange for the chitlins of the pig. The men cooked them out in the yard. I was from up north, and had never experienced anything like that in my life. It was another learning experience that I was able to enjoy.

In the State of Maine you grow apples or potatoes or corn. I was a city girl all of my life and had hardly ever seen an animal on a farm, except for driving by and seeing animals out in the yard. So this was quite an experience. It was fine until the lady there asked me when we had married, and I told her the truth, that we weren't married, and that he had me wear his mother's ring as if we were. She said the only way we could stay there was to get married.

My stepfather altered my birth certificate by putting white-out on the original, and then making a copy of it. I was only 17 and you were supposed to be 18 in order to be married. He took it to the courthouse and we were married. I don't know if I was ever legally married to this man or not. I was a child forced into marriage.

When we got back to these people's house, and told them we had gotten married, they told us we still couldn't live there. I had really loved living there. At night we could hear the Darlington race way.

We left again. We went back to the missionaries from Utah to see if they knew of any other people we could stay with for a few days.

Chapter 14
Darlington, South Carolina
Augusta, Georgia & Atlanta, Georgia

The missionaries knew of another family who took people in. So we lived with these people. They lived across town, and they were very nice. They had some unusual habits. Every time they cooked meals, the cockroaches smelled the food and crawled all over the dishes and stove - it was something else I had never experienced. I was from Maine and cockroaches don't exist in Maine. Maybe it's the cold weather.

They also didn't believe in flushing their toilet paper down into their septic system, and they asked us to throw it into the basket under the sink; they burned the toilet paper in the wood stove. We didn't live there long.

We left South Carolina, and ended up in Augusta, Georgia. My now husband tried to get us a room in a shelter, but they wanted to separate us. They put men on one side and women on the other. My husband wouldn't do that, so we ended up sleeping in our car for a few days until he decided to either pawn everything we could out of the car, or just give it away to the neighborhood kids to get rid of it, because he had sold the car to some man from the shelter. Our car had a broken harmonic balancer, and we couldn't find a replacement because it was so old. It was useless to us.

We had enough money to take a bus to Atlanta, Georgia, where his brother was living with three other men. My husband's brother thought he could find us a place to live. We lived in a one-room apartment off Peachtree Street. The street was called Peachtree Extension. It was behind the Coca Cola plant in Atlanta. When it rained, we had to put a cooking pot under the drip, or we would wake up to a flood all over our floor. You could see daylight up into the roof, and the chicken wire that held the plaster in place wasn't even there.

We went over to the blood donation center around the corner to sell the plasma in our blood three times a week. They injected special anti-bodies into our system so our blood would be worth more. I was fine, but my husband got so sick once that I had to go by myself to sell my blood. I was afraid to do this alone. I had to go to the store by myself and do everything for a few days while he recuperated from that shot.

The Destroying Angel

Some days we would pay our rent and other days we got on the MARTA city bus lines to travel clear across the city of Atlanta into the Black section. We saw a man on the street corner who would reach in under a garbage can lid for a little yellow coin envelope with marijuana in it for sale.

There were several pecan trees behind the food stamp office that we discovered when signing up for food stamps. Every time that a storm hit, it would shake the trees and we would go over and collect the nuts in a box. I shelled them with a can opener, because that's what I had. It passed the time of day - I missed my mother and sister terribly, and tried to keep busy and forget my problems.

We occasionally went to a thrift shop in the neighborhood. We bought a TV once with our money. Another time we bought a hot plate, some dishes, and a kettle and frying pan. We could cook! My husband pulled the bureau into the middle of the room where there was an extra outlet so we could watch TV and cook at the same time. It was a one-burner hot plate. He cooked the spaghetti first and then the sauce.

My husband's brother introduced us to this man. He was a rather heavy-set man that seemed to be rather depressed with his life, so he overate. But he was a very nice, kind man. One day he came over at lunchtime, and we offered him some lunch with us, he replied he

Shirley Turner

had just had a big breakfast. He brought us over a pecan pie another time and had eaten half of it on the way over to see us. He was there until later in the afternoon. After a while he left, so we went to the store.

We had to share a bathroom with two other tenants and I went in and cleaned the tub, then went back to my room to get my clothes. Someone was in there taking a bath in the nice clean tub, and of course they left it dirty, so I had to clean it all over again. I learned to bring my clothes in with me while I cleaned the bathroom real fast.

We came back to our room one day and there was a padlock on our door. The police were called, and the landlord was told he couldn't do this since our rent was all paid up. We decided to ship our stuff to his mother's house and hitch-hike back to Maine.

We couldn't stay at his mother's house long. Spring was just around the corner and my husband was talking like he wanted to leave the state to find a good job, so we ended up in Massachusetts.

Chapter 15

Gardner, Massachusetts &
Bedford, Massachusetts

I was now 18 years old. I didn't have to lie about my age anymore and was working in a chair factory as an inspector. It was a good job, but my husband asked me if any of the men were paying attention to me, and I said they talked to me. That's when he wanted me to quit my job, so I got another job across the street at a spice factory. That was all right with my husband, because only women worked there. I really liked that job.

He had a job at a print shop in Bedford, Massachusetts, which was 50 miles away from Gardner, where we lived. The workers were going on strike, and he asked me if I wanted to work there. I said sure, so we became scabs. It wasn't easy to cross that line. They called us names and threw stuff at us. All we wanted to do was work. I really didn't understand what was really going on at the time. All I knew is that we needed money to survive.

We had a really nice apartment in Gardner, also. I was 2-3 months pregnant. Did I ever have morning sickness! I would have breakfast and vomit, then have my second breakfast, and it actually stayed down. Everyone thought that was kind of weird, but I wasn't hungry at work at least. Gee, we had plenty of money to spend, and my husband actually wanted to work back then. It was a good time in my life. It was such a nice apartment. I really didn't want to leave.

Chapter 16
St. Albans, Maine

I got pregnant in November of 1980. My husband wanted his baby to be born in the state of Maine. He got his income tax check and we went to Maine. He had an old beater station wagon for a vehicle. In fact, that's all he ever drove. We put everything we owned in it and away we went.

We lived in a two-room apartment. I had a pet squirrel that would eat peanuts right out of my hand. My husband didn't work, and we got food stamps. Any money he earned on the side or borrowed from his mother went to pay the rent. He did go to work for the city of Bangor, Maine to pay our rent for a couple of months. They got tired of him coming in to get the town to pay his rent, and asked him if he was looking for a job. He was getting unemployment benefits, and of course he wasn't looking for a job. The town told him he needed to try and get a job or they wouldn't be able to help him anymore.

The landlord was a friend of his mother's, so my husband thought he could get away from paying his rent for a while, but that didn't happen. We lived there until spring. I was 5 or 6 months pregnant. He had bought a tent in Massachusetts, so we went to live in a tent in the woods of St. Albans, Maine.

Oh to live in a tent in the woods when 5 or 6 months pregnant! We had sleeping bags and an air mattress to sleep on. My air mattress had a hole in it and I had to blow it up every night. It would be flat as a pancake the following morning. It made my back ache.

It was very difficult carrying water to our tent, to cook with and wash. It was difficult to take dishes back to the tent to clean them for the next use. The water was a quarter of a mile away from the tent. Even to use the outhouse was a hardship.

His brother had introduced us to the people who owned the property. His brother even stayed there awhile in his Cadillac hearse on these peoples' property.

I tried to keep myself as clean as I could living in a tent in the woods. I would go down to the cistern in the cellar to get water to bathe. We went into Bangor about once a week to bathe at his mother's house.

I was resting in the bed while I could, because he slept in the bed regularly, and I slept on the floor, even being nine months pregnant. Once I heard the water running loudly in the bathroom. I got up to see why the water was running so loudly, and looked around the corner. There was his mother peeking at him taking his underwear off. I immediately went over and closed the door and went back to bed. I was now suspicious of their relationship, and I thought maybe she had abused my husband sexually when he was a child, and maybe that's why he did it to me.

We went back to our tent. I never mentioned it. But I always wondered if it could have been so.

One day we cooked a whole chicken in a pot, and left it in our tent to go to the store to get something to go with it. When we came home there was long shaggy hair in the zipper. The property owner had a long shaggy haired dog. We had pad locks on the zippers and she went right through the zipper. No chicken! Boy, my husband was mad, and he wanted revenge. He broke up a glass juice bottle into almost powder, and bought a nice pound of extra lean hamburger and fed it to her. I felt awful about it, but it didn't bother her a bit. I was so glad it didn't, but I didn't tell him.

My husband's mother taught me to knit while I was pregnant. Each time I would go in to get a bath she would tell me to bring my knitting needles and we practiced knitting. I learned how to make a hat; I wish she could have taught me how to make mittens, though, and sweaters, like she could. They were so beautiful! But maybe someday I will learn.

The months were passing by fast and I was getting bigger all the time. I went into my doctor's office. He gave me some vitamins, because I was anemic. He also asked me if I was going to bottle-feed or breast feed. I told him my circumstances, how I was living in a tent and 9 months pregnant. "So I think I will breast feed, because it would be very inconvenient to get up in the middle of the night to build a camp fire to heat a bottle up." I only gained 10 pounds the entire time I was pregnant. He then told me my due date was going to be July 10, 1981.

On July 8th, I went out behind the tent to urinate before bed and fell down. I went to bed and awoke to a soaking wet sleeping bag. My husband was ready to deliver our baby. He had the scissors and string to tie off the umbilical cord. I convinced him to take me to the hospital. Even the man that owned the property offered to deliver our baby. He had delivered his own children. But I still wanted to go to the hospital, and I'm really glad I did.

Chapter 17
William

I went into the delivery room at 11:00 AM. My baby was going to be a breach baby. The doctor gave me something to turn it around. Our son was born the following day at 5:30 AM, just as the doctor had predicted - July 10, 1981. I was in the hospital for 3 days, and William R. Elliott, our son, was in there an extra 2 days in an incubator. William had jaundice. The doctor said he was living off my liver and he needed to observe him for a couple of days. I still feel that the reason that William was almost a breech baby was because my husband had to have sex with me a week before my due date. I think William turned around to avoid the pounding he was getting in my womb from his father. He couldn't wait a few more weeks. Oh, no it's all about him!

We went to stay at his mother's house. She even let us stay there for the first two days of William's life, before we had to go back to living in the tent.

Our son was 7 days old and sleeping in the tent with us. It was certainly rough. My now mother-in-law had given me a little yellow dish pan, and on nice sunny days I would put some soda bottles in the back of an old car that was on the property, to heat up the water, and gave William a bath in that little yellow pan on the hood of the car. In fact, I still have that little yellow pan, 23 years later. I did this until one day when my husband said that if he didn't get a job soon and into an apartment the state of Maine was going to take our baby away.

I was relieved when he said that, because William was 3 months old now. Winter was going to be here before long.

My husband got a job in Hartland at the leather tannery. First, he worked skinning the fat off of the hides. He got chrome poisoning and broke out in sores on the front of his legs. Then the boss sent him down to where they did the tanning of the leather. He put the hides in a big huge dryer that tumbled them to the right softness. He worked the 2nd shift. Once in a while he would throw a hide out the back door to bring it home. He was stealing.

He worked there through the winter, and I had a stove, refrigerator, and a real bed to sleep in. His mother came to visit one week. She took me out to eat at a little drive in diner place for lunch in Newport. She ordered a lobster roll and told me to get one if I wanted one, so I did. We went home. My husband had made salmon chowder a week earlier, and it was still in the refrigerator. She wanted to eat that, and I didn't. I don't like salmon. She was sicker than a dog for several days. She blamed it on the lobster roll. I tried to tell her that it was the salmon. I didn't eat the salmon and I did eat the lobster roll, and I didn't get sick. She must have used an entire box of diapers to vomit into. She couldn't even get out of bed to the toilet.

We lived there through the winter. A public health nurse came to visit and check our son out to make sure he was doing well. She was such a nice lady. Her husband had died the year before and she still had his clothes. She brought them to my husband, and they fit beautifully. She brought me baby clothes as well; she even visited us while we were living in the tent.

Chapter 18
Lewiston, Maine

We moved to Lewiston, Maine. William was about 9 months old. We had enough money for an apartment without a security deposit. He never paid the last month's rent to the landlord for the deposit. He always took it out in the last month's rent payment. So I had to clean this one.

When we walked into the apartment, there was a puddle in the middle of the floor and it stunk badly. I opened the refrigerator and there was a thawed fish in it, which had defrosted all over the floor. What a nasty smell! I almost lost my lunch right there. There were cigarette butts in the shower. It needed a good scrub down, and I was the one for the job. My mother taught me to clean - not too many other things -but she did teach me to clean. I scrubbed the walls and everything in the place. I had a new baby and he was crawling and getting into everything.

I was still breast-feeding him, and one day my

husband got up off of the couch to change the channel, and I had laid William down in his spot for a moment to tuck everything back into place. The couch we were sitting on was held up by a can of paint on one side and a couple of bricks on the other side. My husband didn't look when he sat down, and sat on William's head. William cried for the longest time. I didn't take him to the doctor. I still blame myself for this, I should have thought about doing that first. My husband said to me, "What did you do that for! That was a pretty stupid thing to do." I should have taken William to the hospital, but we didn't have insurance to pay the bill. To this day I wish I had taken him anyway.

After a few months we moved again. The apartments were always cleaner when we moved out. They were my homes, and I tried to keep them nice and clean.

This time we moved closer to his job; home was an apartment on the 3rd floor. William learned potty training there at a year old. He also stopped breast-feeding there and walked around in his walker. In fact, he got into mischief in his walker, like all children do. William reached into the garbage and pulled out a can. I had an old fashioned can opener that left the top all jagged. He stuck his finger in there, but couldn't get it out. My husband told me to push on the lid instead of pulling his finger out, and it released his finger. It could have taken off his finger.

Another time, we had the oven door open to get a little more heat. William reached into the oven to touch the pretty orange coil in there, and got a burn on his finger.

He had his first birthday, and I made him a chocolate cake with marshmallow frosting. He got that sticky marshmallow all over his face, and wasn't he cute! It was real marshmallow that I cooked in a pan. He always asks for the same cake on his birthday.

I wanted to put William in daycare and go to work, but that was not my husband's plan. He said that babies need their mothers with them while they are growing up. So I continued to have supper on the table and kept the house clean and so forth. We lived there another four or five months, and applied for the new housing development in Auburn, right across the river from his work. It was beautiful, nice, and freshly painted. There was a brand spanking new stove and refrigerator. I couldn't believe my eyes when we walked into it. It was the nicest place we had ever lived.

My husband was making pretty good money working at the print shop. I put William in the stroller and walked across the bridge to see my husband a few times for lunch. Once we went to the Fryeburg Fair, and we had a good time, but my husband got tired and when we left we searched for the car and couldn't find it. He got extremely angry, and after that he started abusing me like he had done to my mother, hitting me and verbally attacking me. He blamed me for anything that went wrong in his life. It was always my fault, no matter where or when it was.

The boys next door to us had a bb gun, and they shot a mourning dove. We took it into the house and tried to nurse it back to health, but it died anyway. At least we tried. One good thing about living there: when my husband was hollering and raving at me, the neighbors heard it. Once, the police were called, but he talked his way out of it.

I was upstairs with William in his walker. I was changing his sheets from the night before. He went over to the stairwell and fell down the entire flight of oak stairs. He had a bruise on his forehead, and the only thing I could do was put ice on it. I knew better than take him to the doctor's office. My husband would have gotten very angry with me for drawing attention to our family. I should have done that anyway. People tell me I shouldn't feel guilty about it, but I have felt guilt over this all of my life. The fall might have injured him seriously, because he has a lot of problems to this day. We couldn't stay in that beautiful housing complex long, because my husband refused to pay the rent or keep a job for any length of time.

Chapter 19
Bucksport, Maine

My husband's brother told him about a woman that would let us stay in her house if we did some chores around her house. So my husband tore the back seat out of our car and put my sewing machine in the middle of the car, on top of the exhaust, and boxes of stuff all around it. The wooden cabinet on my sewing machine caught on fire, because we didn't have an exhaust on our car. It got very hot and smoke was rolling out the windows from the inside of the car. My husband stopped, but there was nothing we could do. We had a load of stuff in the car, and it was a long drive from Auburn to Bucksport. My sewing machine was just charcoal on the top. But it probably saved our lives, because if my husband had put boxes on the exhaust, the inside would have been a ball of fire, and us in it. When we got to Bucksport, we unloaded the car and surveyed the damage, and went back and got another load, but this time he put the back seat in the car.

The Destroying Angel

We got settled into a 2-room attic apartment, a carload at a time. We even tied our mattress and box spring and bed frame to the roof of the car. We sold a lot of our stuff in a yard sale - bureaus and such, but we still had William's crib at least.

We ate a lot of sandwiches and food that was simple to make. But one night the rats got into our bread. We had to keep it in a drawer from then on. I heard the rats crawling on the beams over our heads at night. I was so afraid that William was going to be bitten! It bothered me every night when I went to bed.

Our landlady asked me to make something sweet to eat, so I started to make peanut butter cookies. When I got to the flour part, I opened the metal garbage can lid that didn't fit properly. I saw all of these buffalo bugs in the flour! What could I do, she was sitting right there! I didn't want to make a stink, so I just whipped the cookies right up. I did not have any, of course.

Once we came home and the door was kicked in, so my husband took a 2 X 4 and nailed it across the door. "They couldn't kick that in," he said.

Now I was 17 years younger than my husband, and there happened to be a young man that lived there in the house. He tried to do nice things for me. I didn't encourage him at all; in fact, I tried to avoid him if I possibly could. But my husband got jealous of him. He was walking down the road one day, and my husband pulled the car over and started beating on him and threatened him with a knife and asked for his money. My husband ended up going to jail for two days. The town put me up in a motel room for the two days. Oh, I had television and I could take a shower anytime I wanted, too!

We went back to the house after he got out of jail and still had nowhere to go, so his mother asked her cousin if we could stay with them for a while. They were a little reluctant at first, but they gave in, and away we went to live in Ellsworth, Maine.

Chapter 20
Ellsworth, Maine

We took care of all of our needs without sponging off of his mother's cousins either. In fact, they asked us one day, "Are you folks eating okay, because you don't cook anything here. We wouldn't mind at all if you did cook a meal here." We cooked once in a while.

We were getting food stamps. My husband still wasn't working, though. So we cashed in some of our food stamps to buy gas and such. One day we picked up a local free newspaper, and there happened to be an apartment in Newport, Maine. It was on the third floor and it didn't require a security deposit.

My husband borrowed money from his mother again to get the apartment. We had stored our stuff at his mother's house in her closet, while we lived at her cousin's house. We went to her house and moved it all to our new apartment. We finally a place by ourselves again!

William was three years old by now. He was such a

good help to me and I wished that my mother and sister could see him. I missed them so much, but my husband said they didn't want anything to do with me, or they would have tried to contact me. I didn't know if I would ever get to see them again.

Years later, I found out from my mother that she had contact with my husband's mother regularly. But his mother never told me this. My mother even knew when I was pregnant with my husband's child. Why did all of this happen? I will never really be able to figure it out.

I had gone down to the town to get some assistance and they must have put us on the Christmas list from the American Legion in Newport, because at Christmas time Santa himself brought Christmas presents and a turkey and the fixins - even a Christmas tree! William was so excited to have Santa there! He had never had Santa at his house before, and there he was red suit and all. Santa carried everything up to the third floor by himself. It was truly a wonderful thing they did for us that Christmas.

My husband had to serve time in the Correctional Facility in Charleston Maine. He spent 3 months in there and I couldn't drive. I had to carry groceries and laundry on my back from the store and laundromat. It was not a fun experience. It was winter. I washed clothes out in the sink sometimes - it was so far for me to walk to the laundromat. I started receiving obscene phone calls, and it made me afraid at night. I didn't have any way to protect myself. I would make sure the doors were all locked and I would pull a bed in front of the door. I think that it was the man that lived downstairs. He was doing this to scare me.

I got a phone call from my husband, and he told me that he had a buddy in there, and that his wife came in to see her husband regularly. She lived in Hartland, and that wasn't very far away from Newport. If I paid her a little of the gas, she would pick me up to go in and I could see my husband. So that's what we did twice a week, even in the worst snowstorms. Once the windshield wipers couldn't even keep up with the snow. She would wear a dress with no underwear so her husband could cop a little feel under the table. I didn't do that - it was a little too much for me!

She would sometimes have to get out and clean the windshield or something, dressed like that. She was a good friend for a while. She certainly was a true Mainer!

I was still carrying laundry and groceries on my back in the snow, holding onto William's hand, or he would hang on to my pant leg. He was such a good son, and still is today. It was not an easy life. The only thing I had for protection was a butcher knife that I left on the floor at night next to our bed.

In the spring, my husband's mother bought William a little red wagon to pull our groceries and laundry, and for William to ride in as well. I wish she had encouraged me to learn to drive, because I'm sure my friend from Hartland would have been glad to teach me. I know she had a lot of practice, if she could drive in the snowstorms as she did. There was a car sitting right outside our front door that I could have driven.

When he finally did get out of the Charleston Correctional Facility, I was still getting those calls. My husband answered the phone from then on. Maybe the people downstairs didn't like having someone else up over their heads. But my husband got sick of it, called the phone company. They said there was nothing they could do at the time, and they wanted their money for the phone we bought through them. They wanted us to return it. So one day he was so mad he stomped on the phone until it was just a pile of plastic pieces, and shipped it back to them in a little yellow envelope.

That's when he started abusing our son mentally and physically. It wasn't just me getting hurt by this man now. He snapped and turned into a psychopath any time, anywhere. I never knew from one moment to the next if he would be happy and content. He would suddenly rage like a lunatic.

He made me cut my long blonde hair. I had grown it for years, but it made other men look at me, and that was against all rules in my husband's house.

He was still not working. He was going to the local dump to pick the trash. He even brought home meat from the meat truck that stopped every week. It was out of date meat, but it was the first and only time I have ever had fillet mignon. It was so good; I'll never forget it. We could have all gotten hepatitis or worse. He also found food that a store that had burnt down the previous year had buried in the sand. Our refrigerator was full of beer, mustard, and ketchup. He didn't get any canned goods - they had been frozen and the cans were all bloated up. He sold or cashed in our food stamps to buy gas or drugs or both, and we would have yard sales with anything else he brought home. We picked up a hobby from his brother, which was digging old bottles from a dump that was supposedly closed in 1910.

William went too close to the digging hole and fell into it and broke his arm. After he got his cast off it was his 4th Birthday and we got him a balloon and some toys. We had old iron radiators in the apartment, and the balloon was right over them. William climbed up on the radiator and the balloon moved. He went to reach it, and fell on the radiator and broke his other arm, it was awful!

One day our car window was shot out by a shotgun. My husband suspected that the man whose son he molested found out about it and did it. He sold the car and along with having a yard sale every weekend or so we made enough money to move with. He really wanted to get out of there - I think he feared for his life. He got a truck and kept checking the newspaper for a job. He found one in Brewer, Maine in a print shop.

Chapter 21
Brewer, Maine

It was a very small apartment - even William had to sleep in the living room. How handsome William was for his first day of preschool! He was 6 years and two months old, because his birthday is in July. William only went half a day to preschool. I asked if I could get a job. My husband said that our son needed his mother still. So I stayed home and cleaned house in the morning and took our son to the playground and tried to have fun with him every day. I didn't have any money or very little, or food stamps, so we would get an ice cream or some small treat. I knew that when his father got home it was a totally different atmosphere.

One of the men that my husband worked with dressed up like Santa and went to the orphanages for Christmas. He wanted to spend a little time with William as well, and brought him a present. Our son was really happy, although by now my husband had spoiled the fun by telling him there wasn't a Santa

Claus.

He was always like that - if you really liked something he would destroy it. William and I finally got to the point of not telling him if we really liked something because we knew what he would do to it. He would get home from work and complain about our son's toys all over the living room. One of the guys from work gave William some huge Transformers plastic toys. William really loved them. The living room was our son's bedroom and he had to play with them sometimes. They couldn't stay in that cardboard box all the time.

If I said anything, he would pound on me. It was either our son or me he was after all the time. So I just did everything he would tell me to do, just to keep him from constantly complaining. My husband was buying marijuana from someone at work. If he couldn't get it, he would come after one of us, or throw things, punch holes in the walls, break a bunch of dishes, what ever it was he had, to make a mess for me to clean up.

The lady upstairs asked me one day if I was all right. She had heard him screaming and raving, and probably either William or myself crying. I replied, "Yes," although I was being emotionally and physically abused, and William as well.

One day he told me he was going to go to the head shop to buy some paraphernalia and watch some adult videos in the backroom. He asked me if I would like to go into that place. I said no, I'm not taking my son in there. It was about 175 miles one way. I went and had to urinate badly when I got there. I told him. He said he would only be in there a few minutes. But it turned into an hour. So I wrote him a note and took our son to a restaurant to use the bathroom, and came directly back.

He was furious at me, I shouldn't have gotten out of the car, that something could have happened to me. When I was 15 years old I used to walk the same streets to go to work, and nothing ever happened to me.

He screamed at me all the way home and punched me in my left arm and left leg, so hard that he left bruises the size of softballs. I was as far away as I could get, as close to the door as I could he was still pounding on me while he was driving, and all over the road. People went by blowing their horns. When I got home I went and hid in the bedroom. He never apologized either. I had to wear long jeans and long sleeve shirts in the middle of summer to cover the bruises.

A few weeks later, he bought William a snow sled, and took us to a real high hill. And my son and I went sliding. My husband sat in the car. Who knows what he was doing with all those little kids in sight. But William and I did have fun that day. William still has that sled today.

Chapter 22

Bangor, Maine

We moved not long after that to Bangor, Maine. We lived on the second floor. It was a very big, horseshoe-shaped apartment. William was so happy to have his own room at last! If he wanted room to play with his toys, he certainly had it. His room was at the other end of the horseshoe, so he could really get away from all of his father's anger, and that made me feel a little more secure.

I had a really nice kitchen, with beautiful hardwood maple-stained cupboards. There was a beautiful antique oriental rug in the living room. The old tin ceilings were just lovely. I really liked this apartment! But there always is a "but" to something this nice. A couple of young ladies lived upstairs, who worked the second shift. They stomped up the stairs at night, and turned up the radio late at night. My husband had words with them. They said in return, "If you don't like it move." My husband actually had a job at the time and worked the day shift, so he didn't get much rest at all.

One day we were at the corner store and he met his cousin, who just happened to have a vacant apartment next to him in the house that he owned, from which he had just evicted the last tenants. So we waited a few weeks for them to move out, and we packed up again. This was a duplex, so we pretty much had our own apartment. It wasn't as nice as the last one, but at least William had his own room. There was still constant conflict between dad and his son. My husband complained constantly about toys all over our son's room all the time. It wasn't like he was tripping over them in the living room, which was the case in the other apartments we lived in. William had his own area. But that wasn't good enough for my husband. He thought that a child's room was supposed to be absolutely spotless all the time. He would go into William's room screaming at him.

I don't do well when someone is standing in front of me and screaming at me. Either I start crying or get so angry that I start hollering myself. Maybe that's why my husband would beat me. But I felt I should express my opinion at least in some situations. This was one.

I tried cleaning my son's room every day so that I didn't have to hear about it at night. Then William would complain to me that he couldn't find anything.

So I would get it from both sides. William was 6 years old, so he could have cleaned his own room, and when I did it with him, he would. Then my husband would complain that William was supposed to be doing it alone. I just couldn't win.

One day my husband brought home this magazine that had a lot of ways to grow marijuana in a room. That was his plan when he got his income tax return. So he put cardboard in the windows and aluminum foil on top of that to reflect light. He bought a hydroponic system to grow marijuana. There was a huge revolving light on the ceiling and an automatic watering system that was on a timer. I, of course, had to move into William's room. I ended up taking his bed and he ended up sleeping on a cot, and my husband slept in the kitchen on a foam mattress. There was another advantage to this arrangement; some little girls lived across the alley next door. I'm sure he got his jollies watching them at night. Maybe this was his whole plan: to sleep down there so he could watch them.

My husband still didn't let me go to work. I was taking my son's little red wagon to the laundromat once a week. I got the groceries in it as well. I felt so foolish using that wagon. I know people I knew must have seen me, but he didn't want to spend the time he had off of work to do those chores with me. So I did the best I could.

The Destroying Angel

Then our refrigerator broke down. His cousin didn't want to do anything about it, so we got a new one. My husband threw the old one out in the yard. That made his cousin mad. He, in turn, locked the cellar door to the furnace and electrical box, so he could shut off our power anytime he wanted to, and did on several occasions. The police were called several times. The cousins deliberately tried provoking each other; like they were a couple of kids.

That year, February 1987, my husband's brother died out in California. He was hit by a freight train going 70 miles an hour. The coroner's report was graphic and spared no detail. That's why my husband decided to go up to Garland in the middle of winter. He wanted his brother's bottle collection before his brother's son could get there. His brother had been living there in a tag-along camper trailer during the summer. He spent his winters somewhere warm. The man had dug a lot of bottles out of an old dump that closed in 1910. Our son dug up bags full of them later, after his uncle's death.

There were a lot of bottles there at his camper, at least 2000 or 3000. Some bottles were duplicates. There were small, medium and the large sizes of the same medicine bottle. The old man who owned the land wanted us to clean out the barn first, so that he could use his barn again. We carried all of the bottles back to Bangor and up to the attic, and put them on shelves. It was a lot of work. My husband spent a lot of time up there sorting out bottles. I'm sure he did a lot of peeking out the vent at the little girls, also. It was cold up there and he would leave the door open and freeze the entire downstairs to do this. But at least he left William and me alone for a while.

When spring came we went to Garland again to see what was in his brother's camper trailer. And what a surprise we got! We found his long gray beard in a box that my husband's father had made while he was in prison for murdering someone. There were also a lot of devil worshipping books, and a black hooded cape. The previous summer he had asked us to keep an eye out at the yard sales and flea markets and auctions for a caldron. So now it all fit. When we lived in Atlanta, Georgia, his brother wanted us to go into the House of Witches, and my husband told him right then and there that he didn't think God would want him in there.

I didn't care much for my husband's brother, because he stole his own son's wife away from him and then stole his cousin's wife after that. I was pretty careful around him and I tried not to encourage him. He bought us groceries every time he came to visit us. He wasn't tight with his money. But he certainly did ruin a lot of his family's lives. I'm really glad he never got me.

The Destroying Angel

Before my husband's brother's death, we had gone bottle digging one day and my husband's brother showed up. I tried to apologize for what I had said many years ago to him, which was to speak of the devil. I was referring to the incident in Atlanta, when he tried to take us to a House of Witches. I really shouldn't have said anything like that, but it just came out. I had felt guilty about saying it for many years because it caused a fight between brother and brother.

My husband's brother tripped my husband and he fell to the ground. Then he choked him and pounded his head on the pavement. I tried to get his attention by pounding on his back with my hand, but he didn't even feel that. So I ran into his mother's house and found her cane, and ran out there again. I cracked it over his head. He felt it then, because he got right off of my husband, with both hands ready to strike me. I said to him, "Go ahead - they'll have your butt in the can quicker than you can spit!" He didn't hit me, just stormed into the house, grabbed his duffle bag, and left. The entire fight only lasted only 5 or 10 minutes, but seemed like forever. I was so glad that I got to apologize before he died.

We proceeded to clean the rest of the trailer. That's when we had the shock of our lives. We lifted up his mattress and there was a double-headed sexual device. We just looked at each other with amazement and threw it into the garbage bag. It had been used a lot, because it was almost torn in two on one end. That's when I remembered that he had hair loss on the side of his head by his ears, blotches of it missing. Maybe he had the disease AIDS. Maybe someone knew the kind of person he was, and they pushed him in front of the train. He must have heard the whistle blowing.

Chapter 23
Garland, Maine

My husband's cousin was kind enough to let us move into his apartment house. It was a really nice place, too. But of course my husband wouldn't pay the rent, so we got evicted. We ended up living in his brother's little tiny tag along trailer, where he had lived before he died.

Later we learned that my husband's cousin had committed suicide through an overdose of his prescription drug, lithium. He had taken the entire bottle; they found him the following day. I think he was severely depressed over evicting us from the apartment. He also couldn't seem to get a wife, but his expectations were so high! You know, 38 double D with a 24-inch waist and a 32-inch hip, and, of course, beautiful and smart, with plenty of money as well. Personally, I think he was looking for something that just wasn't out there in real life. At the same time, I really felt badly about his death.

Shirley Turner

My husband's cousin was a good guy at heart. Once he came over and asked me if I would make a molasses cake like his mom used to make him, and to be sure to put lemon topping on it. He hadn't had it since his mother died. I made it the following day for him. He was so happy - it truly made his day!

So here we were, the three of us in a tiny little tag along trailer for the summer. First, we had to tear out everything in the trailer, the smell was so bad. We had to paint everything to get the smell out. We even remodeled it. It was only about a 10 or 12 - foot long camper. It was terrible on rainy days. The three of us in there for a very long time put my husband into a frenzy. Then, one of us would be in the car for the night, or at least for a while, until he cooled off. It was like walking on broken glass every minute. You just didn't know when a shard was going to take your toe off.

My husband built a bunk bed so my son and I could sleep up over him. I remember it was so close to the ceiling that when I rolled over on my side, my hip touched the roof. I was frightened when I woke up, the ceiling was so close. When I look back on it, I'm so thankful that nothing bad happened there, because we couldn't have gotten out of that bunk in a hurry. It was only 15 or 20 inches from the ceiling. If there had been a fire, my son and I might not have made it out of there alive.

I hung our laundry in between two trees to dry. We had food stamps, but very little money. My husband had quit his job at the print shop for the summer. We were cashing in our food stamps to do our laundry. His mother let us come to her house to take showers on the weekends. She gave us a little gas money to get home on. (If you could call it home.) But a good thing came out of that summer. I spent a lot of time with my son. I taught him to ride a bike. There wasn't anything to learn on but a field, but once William got wheels under him that was it.

I wanted to leave my husband so many times! He wouldn't allow me to have even one friend. If someone did want to be my friend, he would try to destroy the friendship. I didn't have any family that cared about me anyway, so I tried to raise William in the best conditions I could.

We had gotten his brother's ashes from California. My husband sprinkled his ashes around this huge chimney his brother had made the previous summer, so that the man who owned the land could finish the cabin. His brother was supposed to be able to come there any time he wanted to stay. We did have the camp to stay in once in a while, but we weren't allowed to live in it. One day we were in there checking on our food and a rat had gotten into the cocoa. We had decided to have a little nap in there, and heard chewing of some kind. A big black rat came out of hiding, and ran across the floor. I screamed. It ran for the chimney and my husband made a fire in the chimney. Afterward he said to me. "You know, my brother believed in reincarnation. Could that have been him coming home to his cabin where he wanted to be?"

I just didn't know what to say. I brushed it off.

The owners of the cabin wanted to rent it out in hunting season. That's why they didn't want us in there. But once in a while we went there. Just to have a few hours out of that little trailer on a rainy day was wonderful.

I never knew when my husband would explode over the smallest little thing. He was growing some marijuana plants down in the gravel pit. He was so stupid. He knew the owner of the land and place, and he knew that his nephew was a game warden. But he thought nothing of it. He got nailed for growing over a hundred plants. The police charged him with the crime. That was the best thing that could have ever happened to William and me, because he had to get an apartment at last, so we moved to Corinna, Maine.

Chapter 24
Corinna, Maine

We moved to an apartment house right across from
a woolen mill, which had been torn down for years. The
apartment was filthy. I scrubbed the floors on my
hands and knees many times to try to get the urine
smell out of the wooden floors. I even washed the
ceiling, it was so bad. But I would have scrubbed any
mess to get a roof over our heads. A shower to use
when I wanted. Not to have to gather wood to cook a
meal over a campfire any longer. What a real treat it
was after being out there in a camper trailer for the
entire summer! I don't mind camping out at all, but
living rough for the entire summer, that was just too
much for me. My husband knew that school was
starting again as well, so our son had to have a stable
environment, or the state would take William away.

While my husband was doing time for his crime, one
week in jail, William and I had the time of our lives. We
could watch what we wanted on TV. Eat, drink, and

stay up as late as we wanted. It was a freedom we had never experienced before. No screaming, raving nutcase at us every minute of every day.

I could smell the chemicals that they used at the woolen mill seeping through the floor. Who knows what it did to our drinking water? They have cleaned the entire operation up, and even removed toxic soil from the area. Men in white hazardous chemical suits tested water. They shut down the entire town's water supply for almost a year, so it must have been pretty bad. At times the odor was so strong the house reeked of the dyes and other chemicals they used in the woolen process.

My husband bought a $50.00 car when he got out of jail. It was an old Valiant that ran like a clock. There wasn't any trunk space at all. When you opened the trunk, you saw two huge tree stumps to hold the springs down in the rear-end. We used it all summer long and sold it to someone who wanted the engine. They got a good one.

William had the neighborhood kids to play with there. William and another boy tore a stove apart in the yard. I will never forget those days. In fact, I saw one of the girls my son used to play with in Wal-Mart the other day. As soon as I saw her face, that memory just flashed back at me. What a nice memory it is!

I went to a teacher's conference and teacher took

me aside and said to me, "Do you realize your son has gone to four different schools in one year?" I said, "I know," and walked away. But I have always wondered what her expression would have been if I had said to her what was really on my mind, which was, "I was the one cleaning every apartment, wrapping and unwrapping dishes. Moving stoves, refrigerators, beds, whatever needed to be done. Because my husband likes to peek at people." He got away with it for many years, without my even realizing he was doing this, until he told me about this little peephole that was in the bathroom. It looked into someone else's kitchen. He told me to make sure that no one on the other side was watching me get undressed. It was all right for him to peep at people, but I had to be careful. I didn't want someone seeing me undress, so I put the towel over the hole when I took a shower.

I made cupcakes for William's school classmates. He was so proud of me! He was 7 or 8 years old and that really meant a lot to him.

We stayed in that house for the winter.

Chapter 25
Winterport, Maine & Brewer, Maine

In early spring, we moved to Winterport, to another apartment, of course. This building had three apartments in it. I was still wondering when my husband would step up to the plate and get a job. But he never did. We lived in the apartment downstairs.

There was a vacant apartment upstairs. At about 5:00 AM, my husband would go up there to watch a little girl get out of her pajamas and into her school clothes. She was probably 8 or 10 years old. In the evening he would go up there again with his binoculars to watch her get out of her school clothes and get ready for bed. After a while, I couldn't stand this any longer. He was doing wrong, violating her by gawking at her. Abusing her, and she didn't even know it. So I left a little note in their mailbox one day. The next day a big thick blanket went up in her window. I was so relieved that she wasn't being violated any longer.

My husband beat me for doing this. It was worth

every bruise I got, to save that little girl from being watched by him. It was bad enough that he did these and many other things to me, but I just couldn't let the peeping go on any longer. After he beat me, I went up to the pharmacy up the street and used the phone to call the Maine State Police.

They took me to William's school and we went to the shelter for battered women in Bangor. We were there 2 or 3 months. I signed up for some assistance to get my own place with William. I needed some clothes from the house in Winterport. So someone took me there to get what I needed, and my husband had left me a note, saying how sorry he was for beating me and how much he missed me. Yeah, right. But William said to me, "I miss Dad." He said that I should go back to him.

I shouldn't have listened, but of course I went back again. I had no family or support system in place. So I did it. I went back to him like a fool. I had gotten assistance from the state to pay the bills. So why would he go to work? Instead, my husband was watching the neighbor's little girl through a peephole he had made that went right into her bedroom. He was even going through her old clothes, finding her underwear, and who knows what he was doing with those.

This time the little girl was 10 or 12 years old. I went

over and told her mother. Of course my husband stopped paying the rent, so that we would have to move again.

This time we moved across the river to Brewer. We moved to a terrible apartment, owned by a genuine slumlord, but with no deposit. I had another filthy mess to clean.

After two years of trying to get a job by riding my bicycle, I managed to finally get a decent job at Eastern Maine Medical Center in Bangor across the river. I started as a cleaning person in the hospital. My husband actually got a job at a local print shop. One of our paychecks would cover the bills. With the other one he bought drugs. So we were still in poverty.

No one was living in the other apartment at the time. There were no children for my husband to spy on. He was working 40 hours a week, so he really didn't have time to do that anyway.

I worked in housekeeping at the hospital. Shortly after I got my job, my husband got into a car accident which killed a woman who worked at the hospital on the same floor where I did the cleaning during the weekends.

I had worked there about 10 months. I said to myself that there had to be a better job in the hospital. So I started watching the job board, and a job did become available. I applied for it and got it. I was so proud of myself that I wasn't cleaning toilets any longer. Not that it wasn't a good job or as important as my new one, but I had always been a cleaning woman. My self-esteem was very low after all of the years I had spent with my husband abusing me and I had a very important job at last.

I learned how to clean and sterilize the surgical instruments for the operating rooms. I was finally doing a job that I could really be proud of - I was actually helping to save someone's life in some small way. In the summer, I would ride my bicycle to work 3 miles a day and home. In the winter, I had to walk back and forth to work. I worked second shift. I felt that my husband could have at least picked me up at 11: 30 at night, so I wouldn't have to risk my life, but that situation just made me stronger. I only got to do that job for 2 years. My husband forced me to quit the most important job of my life. The supervisor didn't want me to leave. I was only allowed to work one more week, so I couldn't even get a reference from them to find another job. I had learned so much in such a little time.

I started to realize that my husband really didn't care about my safety or me at all. Just about how he could use and abuse me.

Chapter 26
Brewer, Maine

We had moved to another apartment on the second floor. And there were some little boys that lived across the street. I didn't catch him watching these boys, but I was working second shift and he was home with William. One day, I could hardly believe my eyes: my grown-up sister arrived on our doorstep. This was in 1992-1993, and I had not seen her for 15 years. She was right there before me. The first thing she said was, "I can't believe you're still with Dad." My reply was, "I had nowhere else or no one else out there to help me get away from him." I got to visit with her for a short time before she had to go home to Florida again.

It was so wonderful to finally see her. She was all grown up by now., and I had missed her for such a long time.

Chapter 27
Brewer, Maine

We moved into a real house in 1993 that rented for $300.00 a month. It was like having our own home at last. My son, at 12 years old, found some friends in the neighborhood to ride bikes with. He was so happy there in Brewer!

A mortician owned the house and he kept the hearse in the garage of this house. It was right next to our living room and kitchen. He was a very nice, kind, man, and until the end my husband used him like he did everyone else.

We went to Pennsylvania to see my Uncle Bob and my mom and sister. While I was in Pennsylvania, William and I walked all over Meadville. We saw the sights. I even went back to my grandfather and grandmother's house to see what it was like as an adult. It was everything I could remember and more. The college students had done a little painting on the house, but it was still the house I remember from my childhood, before the sexual abuse started. It meant so much to me to be able to go back in time. And I would recommend any sexual abuse survivor to do the same, because it was so healing for me.

We had a good time until about the 3rd day when my husband wanted to go home. My family was going to be there the rest of the week, and I wanted to be with them, so my husband started a fight with me. I went to see my mother and sister and they took me to a shelter for battered women.

I realized later why my husband was so anxious to get home. He wanted to see the woman taking a shower at night. But I left a note in her mailbox and she put up something in the window. I got a beating for this from my husband. He broke my ribs this time. It took weeks for them to heal. I have never gotten over the trauma from the beating. I don't think I deserved a beating for anything I have done. My husband was in the wrong for violating that young girl's privacy and he beat a woman who was 25 years old and weighed 110 pounds. I did get some revenge. My husband had a pair of binoculars that I had my son take down the railroad tracks and smash into little bitty pieces.

When we came home, I got a job working as custodian for the Bangor School District on a call in basis. It was money to feed us. My husband had quit his job to stay home and play. He had his settlement from the accident he had earlier. The young woman in the other car died, and they took my husband's blood and found it full of marijuana. They put him on probation and made him attend drug abuse meetings to get off the drugs. But he never did get off of them.

One day, I was doing some cleaning and found a screwdriver in my husband's chair. I didn't really think much of it until I smelt it. You can just imagine what it smelt like. I asked my son about it. He told me he had found it months ago and put it back where it was, never saying a word about it. That's when I realized my husband would have sex with either gender.

My husband was pounding on me one day and the next day he targeted William. On Christmas Eve he said, "I'm sick and tired of this Christmas tree." He threw the tree out that night, ornaments and all. Can you imagine what the neighbors thought seeing it out there on Christmas day? William and I went out a few days later and rescued the ornaments, lights, and tree stand.

Another time, my husband was mad at William over something stupid. He grabbed my son by his ears and proceeded to pound his head on the floor. I ran upstairs and got in the middle of it, to rescue my son. He made William stay in his room all evening that night.

We visited my mother and sister/his daughter in Florida. William was so excited! He had the entire backseat of the 1977 Cadillac we had bought in St Albans for $1,000, just to take to Florida. What a truly nice ride we had going down there! It was a really happy time in our lives. We stopped several times along the way to get souvenirs and citrus fruit and pecans. It was one experience that I will never forget.

My husband could hardly wait to get back home and watch the woman next door showering every night after work. He wouldn't stop even for a drink during the last three or four hundred miles. William was so thirsty when we got home that he went directly to the refrigerator and took a big swig of the milk that had been in there since we had left two weeks earlier. He made the sourest face and went directly to the sink to spit out the sour milk. We all had a good laugh over that.

My son had a friend named John who came over to the house sometimes. My husband actually let him visit. He always told me that we couldn't have any other kids there because he was afraid of being accused of being a pedophile. But now I think he was afraid of himself, that he might lose control and rape another child, as he did to me so many years ago. In any case, our son could never have any other children over to the house. Another excuse was that we smoked dope and he didn't want anyone to know. I really think he was afraid of himself, and what his mind was thinking about.

I know a lot of strange things happened over the years that he just couldn't explain: where he had been and why he had gone there, and so forth. Things just didn't add up the way that he told the story. One day he came in from being away, a true relief for me. During that time I could think and do what I wanted. He came into the house, just furious over something, and slammed the door behind him. The plate glass in the window crashed to the floor. So we had to put a piece of Plexiglas in the frame. The landlord was not happy about it at all.

So many times I had gone to teacher's meetings at school, and would come out crying. The teachers would badger me about what was going on at home that made our son so upset. I tried to get through the meetings and leave as soon as possible. But now I know that I really should have just taken William and left my husband, all those years ago. Our son had so many problems because of the way he was being raised in such a screwed-up environment.

William came home one day with a sterling silver creamer and sugar bowl. I couldn't believe it. He said, "This is for you, Mom. I saw it on my friend's kitchen table and offered his mother a brand-new plastic set in its place. She said sure, I would love to have a brand new set." She didn't realize that she was out-smarted by an 11-year-old. My young man was so smart, with his IQ of 136! How beautiful the sterling silver creamer and sugar set was! It was one of my very favorite possessions. I still have it today.

It wasn't long before it was time to move again.

Chapter 28
Waterville, Maine

We packed everything again. I got ready to clean the next apartment. This time we had moved to Waterville, another city. It happened that there was a woman that took her clothes off with the light on right next door - someone else for my husband to spy on at night.

We didn't live in that apartment very long. We had our stuff stored downstairs and the other tenants were getting into it, so we moved again. But at least we stayed in the same city this time. My son was able to stay in the same school district. My husband had a job in a print shop 40 hours a week; I was working part time as well. My check paid for the weekly rent and his bought some food and drugs; more drugs than food, of course.

Our son spent many hours on his bicycle going through trash for bottles and cans to help us buy food. I just didn't know what we would have done at times, if it weren't for our son picking bottles on his bicycle. He traveled from one end of the city to the other end, just to try and help. I haven't forgiven myself to this day that my son struggled so hard in his life to help his parents who were drug abusers. Such a good son I had, and he was enabling us to be drug abusers. He didn't know it. He was just trying to help us to make it through another day, another meal. He did anything he possibly could to get us food. And that allowed us to get drugs.

He made a little wooden cart. I used to make fun of it and call it a bike cart thing. He would say in return, "Mom, it's not a bike cart thing, it's a trailer." He even painted it red so that people in the cars would see it. He brought more stuff home in that little cart than you can imagine - bicycles, mufflers, bottles, and cans. He collected anything he could make a dollar on. He eventually got enough bicycles together to sell them as a lot to a bicycle dealer he found in *Uncle Henry's Swap and Sell Guide*.

I truly think that God gave me a guardian angel of my very own. My son was always there when I needed to talk to someone, he was truly my best friend, and always will be. He saved every single penny that he could as well to someday be able to buy his own car or "wheels," as he said. He was going to do something with his life, rather than get high on drugs. And I was so proud of that, that he had a plan at thirteen years old.

I had a job clear across town working in a nursing home in the laundry. I hoped that one day I would get a job in housekeeping, I rode my bicycle back and forth every day. It didn't matter what the weather was, I had to get to work. My husband still didn't teach me to drive. I went through four driving permits before I finally got my license, because my husband would sit next to me while I was driving and scream at me that I was doing this wrong and that wrong. I let one after another permit run out instead of trying to get my license.

I did get my license many years after that though. It was one month before my son got his permit at age 18. It was strange being the oldest person in the driving school. But at least I finally had my license, and the only reason my husband let me get it was that he was losing his eyesight and wouldn't be able to drive anymore. He had to have total control of me just as long as he possibly could.

One evening our son came home excited. He told his father and me that out in front of the local charity donation box there was a lot of stuff sitting on the ground. There was so much that they couldn't get it all into the donation box. My son wanted us to go and look at it. Well, I wasn't really interested, but my husband said, "Go down there with him and see what's there." So I went anyway.

We took our bicycles and away we went. There were two boys picking over the stuff, so I thought I would check it out too. The two boys ran over to the police station, which was right across the road. They told the officers that we were picking those donation boxes. They were doing it first. I am not trying to blame anyone else, because now I know that it was a bad thing I was doing. But at the time, I really didn't think there was anything wrong in doing it.

The officer came over to where we were and I started running, but my son just went and hid. The officer came after me. He hollered at me, "Stop or I will shoot." So I stopped, right in my tracks. He came charging at me with all of his weight. He was 6 feet tall and probably 250-300 pounds. I was 120 pounds, 5 foot 4 inches. Oh, he hit me just like a linebacker hits one of his opponents. It hurt me so badly! He turned me over and I bit his hand and grabbed his crotch. Mistake number two.

My son jumped out of the woods and started kicking the police officer. The officer called in for more back up, and he sprayed me with pepper spray. Believe me, nothing could have been worse than that!

I spent two days in jail and my son was put on probation. The police officer came in to see me and held out his lip stating, "See what you did to me, you gave me a fat lip." I told him, "I didn't do that, my 13 ear old son did that to you." He didn't believe me and stormed out the door.

My husband told me later that the officer came to him and said the exact same thing. I couldn't believe what my husband's reply to the officer was. He told him, "It sounds like she was just trying to defend herself, that's what it sounds like to me." After all of the years I had spent with him being and saying such negative terrible things about and to me, he actually said something positive and supported me. I wish it could have been in some other form instead of against a police officer.

I did nothing but cry for two days in jail, and my body was sore from the linebacker hit and the pepper spray. To top it all off, I was fired from my job. But I did learn valuable lesson, because I didn't understand I was stealing. I really was, and I will never do anything to put myself in danger of being put in jail again. Of all the terrible things that have happened to me, that was the worst. It was truly embarrassing and degrading and nothing is worth that, free or not. I will never do anything to put myself in that position again. The money that my son had saved ended up paying my fine for being in jail. I can't believe how stupid I was! And William had to spend the money he had worked for so hard on my foolishness.

Instead of keeping his job, and keeping things together, my husband quit his job. I asked his mother years earlier about her life with her husband, and he did the same thing. When things were just starting to get better for them, he would quit his job and that is pretty much what my husband did as well. Only this time, it had gone from bad to worse.

He stopped paying the rent and we ended up having to move again. Things were really going well for William. As much as our son pleaded to stay in Waterville, my husband insisted on moving to an entirely different area. Over and over again this happened to us, ruining friendships and relationships. In Waterville, William was getting good grades and there was not a complaint from school. My husband had no regard for him or his life at all. I feel he should have considered our son's opinions and life a little more. He was selfish and thought of no one but himself. William begged his father to stay in Waterville. He had a girlfriend and a new start in life. It would have meant so much to William! But it was all about my husband. Nothing ever mattered. Only what he wanted mattered.

Chapter 29
Bingham, Maine

This time we moved to Bingham, a very small town. It did have a tiny little Surefine supermarket.

Bingham was way up north deep into the woods. Our son came home with straight A's for the most part. So, academically, the move didn't affect our son too much. But he lost all his friends again. That was bad enough.

We stayed there for about a year. We had our share of disasters. I broke my foot on the cement stair in the garage. My husband tried to commit suicide by going into the garage and running the car, trying to asphyxiate himself. I called the police and he got upset with me and ran off into the woods. Our son chased after him.

I had to face the police when they came to our door expecting to save my husband's life. That day he taught our son a "survival skill," by hiding in the ditch so the police didn't find him. He was teaching our son that the police were the enemy.

The doctor took notice and gave him medicine to help him with his depression. In fact, they started working with all of us, to treat all of our needs. We fell through the cracks in the city, but here in the country we were helped at last. We never moved to a city again.

William still missed all his friends from school in the big city. This time, instead of fighting with other tenants or neighbors, my husband fought with the landlord. So we had to move again. There was only one thing different this time. My husband had applied for his Veterans Benefits. I hoped we would have a more stable life at last. It's just too bad that he couldn't have gotten benefits earlier to give William more stability.

We moved clear across the state.

Chapter 30
Corinna, Maine

We moved into a tiny little house in Corinna all by ourselves, which was nice. There wasn't any one for my husband to peek at through the windows. I did one thing differently, now. I finally spoke up and gave my husband an ultimatum: He needed to get us a permanent place for us to live. I told him that if we didn't get a home and stop moving every 3 months, I was going to leave his sorry butt after our son turned 18.

I had not stood up to him very many times, so he knew that I meant it. Even when he had me cornered and was beating me, I never fought back or hurt him. I never could hurt him. I'm not like that. So, for the first time we actually lived in peace with our landlord and neighbors. I couldn't believe it. It was as if my husband, after 16 years of marriage, had finally grown up and faced that he had responsibilities to his wife and his son.

Shirley Turner

We had a vegetable and flower garden there. We mowed the lawn together. William was in love with a girl from school. He rode his bicycle 7 or 8 miles back and forth to be with his girl in Hartland on the weekends. William truly loved her. In the end, I found out what an important relationship William had with this girl. I can remember how important it was for him to be there every single weekend. I don't think he missed one single weekend even in the winter months. She is a very kind and caring person to me, even more than some of my own family members.

I say this because I talked to one of them about something rather confidential and they ran right back to the person and told them. I guess it's how you're brought up in life. What your morals are. I would never betray anyone, especially a family member, but apparently some of my family members just don't care about anyone but themselves. I was talking to this particular person and they were watching television while we were talking, and didn't even hear what I was saying to them. Apparently they didn't want anything to do with me, and that's just fine with me.

One day we went to a house where they had border collies for sale. I had never had a dog in my life nor had William. So we took one home.

About two weeks later, I went to an auction and broke my foot in a hole on a cement floor. You'd think

109

I would have learned about cement floors from the last broken foot! For one whole week my husband took care of me. Then, he told me I was on my own. I wrapped up my foot with the cast on it in a bread bag and took the puppy out when it needed to go. This was during the winter. I could have fallen and broken the other foot, but I didn't.

Spring came and we moved again. Even now, every time I drive by this particular house, I have a memory of my son out in the yard plowing snow with this little hand truck, made into a snowplow. It is so vivid in my memory that it's almost like I'm still sitting there watching him from the window. In my recollection, he is wearing a coat that he got when he was about 10 years old, and it is almost too small for him. When I bought it for him, it was way too big for him, but that's the one he wanted. He knew that it might be a very long time before he got another brand-new coat. He knew I had worn the winter coat I had gotten when I was 18 until I was 35 years old. It's like the song *coat of many colors my momma made for me*. Now I understand what the song actually was talking about.

There were still many fights between my husband and my son. On one day, my husband would deliberately start a fight with our son, then the next day it would be my turn. I think he was doing it to get attention from the other person, or to make the other person look bad in their eyes. I think he was trying to turn William and me against each other. I know how jealous he got when I would take just a few minutes and spend time with William. I guess I was just supposed to ignore William and spend every waking moment with my husband.

My husband wasn't like a normal man. He liked to do a lot of things women do, such as knit and crochet; he also did some sewing, cooking, and baking. He even knew all about flowers and plants. I didn't even realize that men enjoyed sports, because he didn't like sports at all. Perhaps it was because his mother was there and his father was not there. Maybe that's why he was screwdriver crazy. But William wasn't like that at all. Our son was a manly kind of man. He liked girls, cars, wrestling, and bicycling. And foremost, he liked making money to buy his girlfriend things.

Chapter 31
Dexter, Maine

About 6 months later, my husband found a nice old farmhouse about 20 miles from where we lived in Corinna. It was an eight-room farmhouse. William loved it. He had his own room upstairs, and it was not a little closet to sleep in, either. It was a real room, away from his dad. I thought this might be it - William and his stuff would be out of sight. My husband wouldn't be able to see it unless he went up there specifically to find something to complain about. And he did, many times. Sometimes it made me wonder if he just thrived on conflict.

The rooms all had hard wood floors, with wide pine boards. They were so pretty after I stained and varnished them! They were easy to clean - all I needed was a dust mop. You could tell the last time the place had been painted was in the 1940s. The lime green paint of the living room said it all. A beautiful old Glenwood parlor stove in the living room kept us all nice and toasty for a few years. There was even an old summer kitchen, and the back part was the woodshed, which was built in 1816. It was truly a historical place.

It was really neat to go out there and think about how their lives must have been at that time. We moved there in August of 1998, a year before William graduated from high school. I hoped that we would be able to stop moving at last. I hoped I wouldn't have to clean up someone else's filthy mess again.

A little old lady had lived here until her last days. The people we bought it from told us if we put a deposit on it, we could make the final payment the first of the month. It even had 10 acres. I was so happy at last! I planted a lot of flowers to come up in the spring. And each year that I lived there I planted more. I even planted blueberry bushes, and my husband put in some fruit trees. There were already some currant bushes out back and I made currant jelly one year. Oh, it was just delicious!

The following year we went up to Jackman to pick wild strawberries to make jam. We did that almost every year. In this way, we would have a little treat in the middle of winter. William found an old rock quarry across the street with milky quartz stone in it. I asked him to bring me over a few rocks to make a rock garden. "I'm right on it, Mom." He took his red wagon over and came back with a load for me. Such a good son I have! They were so pretty out front for everyone to see.

That Christmas we went on our own land and cut a Christmas tree. What a nice feeling it was, to do this on your own land.

William was getting A's and B's in school. Life was good for a while. We finally had a stable life. I signed William up for Social Security Benefits. He qualified since he was under 18. At that time, if a child with a disability was under 18 and registered with the Veteran's Administration, and had a parent who was a veteran, the parent could receive money until the child turned 21. William had many social and physical problems. This resulted from all of the abuse at his father's hands. By now, William had developed PTSD. So William received money from Social Security.

My son received a retroactive check from Social Security, and my husband spent it on things for himself. He purchased a wood splitter, chipper and a bush hog. William got nothing to start his own life out with. He said to me, "That's okay, mom. At least Dad's happy. I will do it on my own. And he will get some exercise outside which he really needs. So he can lose a little weight. And his diabetes won't be so bad." William thought of everyone .

I still had my border collie puppy. She was growing up pretty fast. She loved all of the cats next door. Trixie would sit in the hallway and cry to them to play with her. So we got a mixed breed Rottweiler and named her Daisy. We taught them to go out to the woodpile and get the wood for the wood stove. Trixie carried it in her mouth and loved doing it. But Daisy didn't really care for it. When they carried in the wood, it saved me an extra trip out there.

William bought an Oldsmobile out in Hartland for $300.00. I teased him about it because it didn't run half of the time. I called it his brown lemon. His girlfriend talked him into buying it. It did run for a couple of weeks. His father told me he was going to give his old Ford F150 pickup truck to William as a graduation present, but my husband was greedy. He made William pay $200.00 for it. William wanted a truck and it certainly lasted a lot longer than his brown lemon.

I was making a vegetable garden and there was a huge rock right in the middle of it. William got a shovel and dug all the way around it and put a long chain around it and hauled it right out of there with his Ford F150 pickup truck. It left a huge hole. My husband continued to rototill it until it was level and I put cow manure on it. That year we had the most wonderful garden around, although it was pretty stinky! Even my neighbor called up and asked what stunk so badly over there. "I thought the farmer down the road only had a stink like that!"

The Destroying Angel

He brought junk home to recycle. His dad was the one to take it apart, sort it, and box it up. William took it to the recycling center down in Oakland, and they split the profit. It seemed to me that his dad got the easy part, because William had to buy the gas, collect the junk, and even help his dad tear it apart and sort it. But at times it really went well between them. At other times, living with my husband was like living with a nut case.

With the last of the money in the bank, my husband bought a Chrysler Imperial Gold Crown. It was a beautiful car. It had torpedo taillights. The interior needed to be redone, but it was really cool to ride around in. My husband got tired of it and it sat up in the field for a year or so. Then one of them took the dashboard apart, and that was that. It didn't start in our yard again. But I saw it about 6 or 8 months later in a restaurant parking lot, so that wasn't the end of it.

My husband bought a gold dodge pickup. Now that was another story all in itself. My husband saw an ad in *Uncle Henry's Buy it Swap it Guide*. He drove to Pittsfield to look at this 4-wheel drive Dodge Ram pickup truck. It was a big old beast. William was taking mechanic classes in school, and the first thing he did was look at the frame. He said, "Dad, you don't want this truck. It's got a broken frame." I stayed in the car the entire time because my job was to get the car home if he bought the truck. I could hear William keep telling him, "no, don't buy this." But my husband he never listens to anyone but his mother. He paid $900.00 for a truck with a broken frame.

We started out down the Interstate, going about 45 miles per hour. My husband decides to jam the truck into 4-wheel drive without stopping and unlocking the locked hubs - and boom! There goes the 4-wheel drive! So he bought a gold lemon with now a broken 4-wheel drive. He didn't even get it home before all this happened. He spent another $250.00 on getting the 4-wheel drive fixed, and blew it out in a week's time. But it was a good old yard truck at least. He took our trash to the dump in it, too. But for that $1150.00 we certainly could have taken our trash in the car.

One day, I twisted my ankle and I wanted to go somewhere on the farm. William just picked me up and carried me where I wanted to go. He said to me, "Gee, Mom, you're so little!" He was young and really strong from all that junking and at that time, I weighed only 120 lbs. No matter what he was doing, if I needed help, William was right there, from the time he was 3 years old, when he was washing dishes with me in the sink. The following year I had a garden with 10-foot tall corn growing in it. I had so many tomatoes I had to start cooking and freezing them before they got out of hand.

Chapter 32

Dexter, Maine

My mother and sister had come all the way from Florida to visit us and see the house. My sister could hardly believe my 10-foot tall corn - and the Chrysler Gold Crown Imperial. My husband tried to start it to show it off a little bit, but it wouldn't start. My sister had her movie camera going and commented that there were two big greens in her view. My husband, her father, had a big green t-shirt on at the time. She said to me later that at the time she said to herself, "I shouldn't have said that." She knew that that my husband/her father could have gotten mad about it, because he had abused her verbally when she was a little girl. This shows how much abuse we all suffered at his hands. I never knew when my time bomb husband was going to explode.

My sister, mother and niece were only there for a week, but we did the usual tour. We went down to Rockland to the Lobster Festival. I wasn't that impressed with it, but my sister was. Once you've seen it, that's it. But every year we had to do the same old things with her. There is so much more here in the State of Maine - they don't call it Vacationland for nothing. But on the way to Rockland, my husband and son had a quarrel in the car. We were carrying six people. It was over something stupid, of course.

I remember being out in the yard picking flowers with my niece, while my sister filmed it. What a nice memory it is for me!

A few months later my husband went up to my son's room and kicked the door in. He threatened to do more damage if he didn't clean his room up. My husband told me to call the police. I did what I was told. My son tried to get out of the house and away from my husband. He had made it down the stairs and to the back door. When there was a knock at the door. It was the police.

My husband asked the officer if he had a gun, and the officer replied, "No." My husband's reply was, "They might as well have sent Santa Claus as you." I was relieved that the officer didn't bring a gun to kill my son with. But why would my husband want the officer to have a gun, to kill his own child? By then, William had jumped through a window and was gone into snow that was 8-10 inches deep, in his blown-out sneakers and with only a quilted flannel shirt on.

The Destroying Angel

William was on his way to his girlfriend's house after dark. It was a good 20-mile walk. The deep snow made it even worse.

We waited for the police to catch our son. But he was too smart for them. Dad had taught him skills to avoid the police when we lived in Bingham. He walked through the woods beside the road, not on the road. My husband got impatient waiting for the policeman and got in his car that had a squeaky fan belt. We started down the road and out popped William. I was so relieved that we had him safe and sound and that we were on our way home. On the way back to the house, my husband stopped and let the officers arrest my son. It took 6 officers to hold my son down and put the cuffs on him, he was so strong.

William was put into a psychiatric facility for two weeks. The first week William couldn't even call us. And when he did, he told me that he hadn't had a bowel movement since he had been there. He said that the doctors were very worried about this, and treated him with all kinds of laxatives with nothing working. My husband suggested prune juice. That worked. He called me later and he could hardly talk, he had to go so much. I was really relieved and I know he was also!

My husband and I had quit using marijuana for three years and that's why we were a little stricter with William, I guess. He even told me that he was really proud of us that we weren't using anymore. But my husband went back to it after the 3-year mark. I made it to four years. But all that year my husband kept saying to me, "Here have a hit, it won't hurt you." So, after the fourth year, I gave in. He was still spending $800.00 a month with or without me smoking. He wasn't buying anything else, so I gave in. It was the worst thing I could have done. My son was let down again.

My husband got $3200.00 a month in benefits, and spent $800.00 of it on marijuana, and then gave me $100.00 and told me, "Here's the money for groceries this month and anything else you want for yourself." There wasn't anything left for me after I bought the groceries!

I can't tell all negative things about my life with my husband and son. There were good times. We went out to eat and to the local auctions or to an estate sale. In fact after 20 years of living with this man, he bought me my first diamond at a yard sale for $100.00. I was amazed that he spent that much on me. I even got a washing machine after 13 years. I just wish that he could have gotten along better with his son, but they were too much alike for that.

My husband sat around watching television a lot and doing drugs. He wanted William to move his truck one day. William said, "Dad, I'm loading it up, so I need it to stay there a little while longer." That wasn't the answer my husband wanted to hear. He got into his own truck and was going to push my son's truck out of the way. William got between the trucks and said, "No, Dad, no." My husband revved up the motor and started towards William. I couldn't stand this! I jumped in the middle of both trucks. My husband said, "Get out of the way, Shirley." I said, "No. You're not going to hurt William."

William had a huge roof rake that Dad made and gave to him for his own roof. William took it and swung it right through my husband's windshield. My husband backed off then and went down to the police station. William and I laughed - it was just like a dog whimpering away. The police couldn't do anything because I wouldn't side with my husband. He was really mad. But I went upstairs for the rest of the day and he went to bed. A few weeks went by and the trash was piling up, so my husband called the glass company to replace the window. He finally took the trash to the dump.

Chapter 33
Florida and Dexter

We decided to take a trip to Florida. So we drove down there. My mother wanted some milky quartz. William went right over to the quarry and got some for her, and put it in the back seat of the Oldsmobile my husband had bought a few months earlier. We stayed at my sister's house. We slept on her fold out couch. We had a good time while we were there. We went to the flea market and to the Space Observatory Museum. I almost made it to the Ripley's Believe It or Not Museum in St. Augustine, but my husband said, "No. We're not going in there." It made me sad, I wanted to go so badly, but it didn't matter to my husband. What he wanted to do was the important thing.

We had to leave Florida early because my husband had run out of marijuana, and that was more important than anything. We hardly stopped anywhere on the way back to Maine. I managed to talk him into getting a bag of oranges and pink grapefruit, and even a southern ham. He later wished he had gotten another one, because it was so good.

My son was going to Head Trauma Therapy. He had performed at the Special Olympics in Bangor. He was so proud - he won several blue ribbons and talked to his favorite sportscaster in the whole world, Tim Throckmorton. I was very proud of him. I put all of his medals in a display case for him. He said, "No, Mom, you keep those. I don't have a place really for them where they won't get broken." I am so glad he made me keep them now.

A week after his 18th birthday, my husband wanted William to move out of the house. I couldn't believe it! My son wanted to stay right there for the rest of his life and that would have been fine with me, but not with his dad. Our neighbor had an old trailer that he wanted to get rid of. William asked the man if he could have it. "Sure, as long as you get it moved yourself."

There was no water, no electricity, just a wood stove, and William was as happy as he could be. If he needed anything else, he would come down to the house. But that still wasn't good enough for my husband. He wanted to be able to use William whenever possible, but he did not want him around at any other time.

William was working with a social worker to try and

learn how to deal with the situation with his father. I helped him get a loan from a program for low-income people to buy a newer trailer. It wasn't brand new. But you should have seen that little happy face when it was delivered! He could not even wait for them to bring it up the driveway and set it up. He had to go inside it while it was in the middle of the road and just check it out. I was really surprised to hear my husband say, "Well, we need to take out a second mortgage to get him a well and septic." I almost fell on the floor with astonishment that my husband thought of William for once before he did himself!

William didn't want to leave me with his father because of how mean his dad was with me. You would have thought things were going to be fine now, with William moved out of the house. But anything my husband could find to bicker about with either one of us he did, no matter how small. I loved having my son up there in the field. Any time I needed help he was right there for me.

By this time, William was all set up in the field in his almost new trailer. He had a well, septic, the whole works right there. But his dad ordered him off of his property. What a stupid mistake that was in the end!

So William got a piece of land, well and septic 20 minutes away from us, on a very busy highway. At least he could make a mess or do anything he wanted to, without his dad squawking at him.

William was going to this woman for counseling. In fact, she helped my son get the land that he had his trailer on. Another lady gave William a solid cherry dining room tablehop - it was beautiful. She told William that he could store it at her house until he got settled in. But then she wouldn't give it up, until we all went there after it one night. William argued with her and she finally gave in. My husband at the same time said to me, "I need to take a crap," and he came up with this plan to put it in her mailbox. We all laughed. But sometimes things come back on you. My son said he got some obscene phone calls after that.

William was still there at our house quite a bit, because he was afraid his father would beat me or kill me. My husband had threatened it many times and he had seen his rages many times. But anytime my husband had something he couldn't do, he would call up William. Then, after he got him to do what he needed, he would fight with him, to make him go home.

Thanksgiving was fast approaching. My husband bought a pork roast. Oh I love roast pork! We still had the old wood stove in the kitchen. He put the wood right to it. It hadn't been used in years and was full of soot. It started roaring inside, and we had to call the fire department. They went right by the house at first.

No one had ever needed them out there. The people who had lived here before knew enough not to start a big fire in the chimney, because it hadn't been cleaned in years. So I called them again, and told the dispatcher to tell them to back up.

We had a cleaning done that day, and it took almost all afternoon. My husband put the pork roast in the oven like he should have to begin with, and we had a late Thanksgiving. So did the firemen! I will always be thankful that they were there when we needed them. The next Thanksgiving, November of 2001, we had a turkey.

But it was on the next day that the worst thing happened. My husband was whining that his sciatic nerve was bothering him. He wouldn't go to Togus to have a doctor examine it, or give him something for the pain. He just wanted to lie around the house and complain about it. So I said, "Well I'm going - I need some medicine. I'm totally out of it." And I said, "William wants to go with me." So we hopped in the car and away we went.

My husband made a big deal out of it with the police, but we got home okay. William said, "Mom, you know what he's going to do. He's going to drag you in there and abuse you while I'm out here. And then call the police on me. Then have me put in jail like he always does." I said, "I know, William, and I hate it. I won't call the police on you for him anymore, and doesn't it tick him off!"

When we got home, my husband was in a fury as usual when something didn't go just the way he wanted. He would do anything he could to make the situation his way or no way at all.

People have told me that his mother spoiled him so much. And she gave him this Peter Pan Syndrome. I know he's got something wrong with him, something that no other woman would have stood as long as I did.

It was almost dark when we got home. William and I had a wonderful day. I had money, and gas in the tank. We went to one of William's favorite restaurants, Denny's. We drove up almost to the house, and William said, "Stay here, Mom, I will be right out." So I waited on the other side of the road and watched to see what would happen.

William went in the back door and went to our bedroom to get my pills and my dog Trixie. He brought them out to the car, and went back to find the gun. I had told William that I was worried that my husband might kill himself. I should have realized that he was too selfish and arrogant to do that, but I was afraid. So William went to my nightstand next to the bed. My 9-millimeter handgun was gone. William started to leave, and my husband hit him in the head with a huge flashlight that my mother, his ex-wife, had given him

128

for Christmas a year earlier.

William didn't even think of what or who hit him. He turned around, and, wham! hit right back between my husband's eyes. William headed for the door to leave again. My husband pulled the 9-millimeter from out of the cupboard, and fired at our son. Luckily, the gun jammed the first shot, and my son managed to get into my car and got away. But my husband unloaded the rest of the clip into my car, one in the tire, and one almost in the gas tank.

We went directly to the police station. Our neighbor called the police upon hearing the gunfire. My husband called the police on himself. He fled to a friend's trailer, and the police surrounded the trailer. One by one, they got everyone out, and then went in after my husband. They chained and shackled him and sent him to jail for shooting at his own son. He spent the next three years in prison.

William and I had the time of our lives. William had anything he wanted to eat, drink, and be merry. He saw an ad in the local *Uncle Henry's Buy, Sell and Swap Guide*. There was a 1978 Oldsmobile with a three fifty rocket engine for sale in Bradford for $350.00, and William wanted to go and see it. There was some rust, but for its age it was well taken care of. It needed a tune up really bad. But William drove it home. He said, "I will work on it for you, Mom." So we started spending some money on it, and on other things as well. I had full possession and control of my husband's $3200.00 monthly veteran's check. Boy, did I do some shopping! If William needed anything he got it. We had so much freedom! We could stay up and play cards until midnight if we wanted to. We could watch anything we wanted to on television. It was like we were set free, out of our little cages. There was so much time to do what we wanted!

We didn't have a Christmas tree that year, but the presents sure did make up for it! My mother and sister, who were his ex-wife and daughter, kept in touch with me. And William went to see his dad in jail. He told me that his dad looked just like a raccoon from where he hit him after my husband hit William with the flashlight. I know that it hurt William to see his father that way. He was only in jail a couple of weeks and then went to prison for four years. He got good time, and was released in three years.

In the new year of 2002, my sister wanted me to come down and visit her in Florida. She wanted William to come also but he said, "No, Mom. I will watch the farm and take care of the dogs and so forth." So I started to get ready. I filled the freezer with things he liked to eat, along with any junk food I knew he would like. I had the oil tank filled. My car was full of gas. I gave William some money just in case he needed something. On the 1st day of February, I got a ticket and my luggage packed. And away I flew to Florida!

My sister said I needed a little break after all that happened. I had a good time in Florida. I bought presents for William and my family, too. I went to the flea market, and The Golden Corral, my favorite restaurant. I spent all my money, so I had to come home to Maine again. I got home on February 12th, 2002, late in the day. William picked me up at the airport, and I was glad to get home. It's nice to get away but really nice to get back to your own place.

William wanted to go to his friends in Corinth to get some tires the next day. We arrived home pretty late in the day, almost dusk. My life was about to change for the better at last.

Chapter 34
Paul

That's when my life had meaning and contentment. I had such a good son and I was about to meet the most wonderful man in the entire world. (Well, he is to me, anyway. He tells me that he's just normal, "I'm not anything special, Shirley.") But he is totally different from my husband. His name was Paul and I could hardly wait to talk to him. I never saw anything so exquisite as Paul in my entire life! Paul's buddy was with him to change a dump truck tire. His buddy came into the house right after me. I thought he was going to tear off my clothes with his eyes. He started telling me all about his 100 acres and big Veterans Benefit check and all of his construction machines, and on and on about all that he had. But all I could see was another Vietnam Veteran with PTSD. Someone had told me not to get another one like that.

I finally got enough courage to let the little guy down. Because out in the yard was Paul. Just what I had needed for so long. So, I said, "Who is that other guy with you?" And his little face just crashed and sank right down to the floor. His reply was, "Oh, you mean Paul."

I said, "Oh, tall Paul."

He then asked me if I wanted to meet him. I said, "Well - yes!"

He said, "I will go out and get him for you." It was a few minutes before he even told Paul. He was so discouraged with his own little self - losing the girl again - that it took him a while to even tell Paul I wanted to see him. But Paul finally came in. And my son's friend, being the gentleman that he is, asked us if we all wanted to have popcorn and sodas.

I was lucky enough to share my bowl of popcorn with Paul, and to this day when I eat popcorn with him it's such a good memory for us both! He was so handsome, and that's saying nothing about the size of those rubber boots he had on. He even had a mind. I could hardly wait to see him again. But I kept my cool the best I could and when we were all through and William was ready to go, Paul and I exchanged phone numbers. It was February 13, 2002. I was hoping he would call on the 14th, but he said, "I will call you in a couple of days." He was such a stud. He finally called on the 15th. I wondered what he had done for Valentines Day?

The Destroying Angel

Paul said he had done nothing, just stayed home alone. I was a little bit discouraged at this point, because I wanted to see him as soon as possible. But he made me wait. And that's what he told his buddies, that you should always make her wait for you to make the move. But at least he called. So we made a date for the 15th of February. He told me to follow Route 16 South into Lagrange, and take a turn on Mill Street and it's the first trailer you come to. Well I took Route 16 all right I just went north, and ended up in Dover-Foxcroft. Totally wrong direction! I turned around and ended up going right through LaGrange, to another town. I finally saw a sign that told me exactly what to do. I was only an hour late. But all of Paul's brothers were there telling him, "She's not going to show." Boy, were they all surprised to see me!

I don't like to drive at night and it was raining and I was in a part of the country I had never been in before.

I stood there shaking all of their hands. Paul's mom is 6 feet tall, Paul's brother is 6 feet 8 inches tall, and another brother is 6 feet tall. Paul is 6 feet 5 inches tall! Here I am, only 5 feet 4, and they're all standing around me! I felt like a little small mouse, and these big cats were here to see what little morsel Paul had caught.

I told them all about what had happened to my family, how my husband was going to be in prison for four years for shooting at our son (My ex-husband divorced me while he was incarcerated), and Paul still wanted to go out with me. I was so happy he did! We said our goodbyes, and we were on our first date. He wanted to take me out to dinner. I was so excited it was I of all people he wanted to be with. I was just shocked that such a nice, kind, smart, good-looking man as he would want to be with me, and so happy he did.

I guess it was love at first sight for me. But I had to find out what Paul felt. I had fish for my dinner, and Paul had meatloaf. When I go out to eat, I always have something that I can't make at home. We went to see a movie afterward. I did exactly what my son told me not to do. But I was so afraid that Paul would get away from me before I even got to get to know him. I said the heck with what my son said, which was, "Don't have sex on the first date, Mom. He won't respect you and want to keep you." I had never dated before, so this was all new to me.

So instead of Paul going home to his own place, he came back to stay at my home. I immediately asked him if he wanted anything more to eat, drink or be merry with. He said, "No, I'm all set. I will watch a little TV with you though."

Paul started caressing me all over, and I asked, "What are you doing to me that is making me so excited?"

His reply was, "It's foreplay. You've never had

foreplay before?"

I said, "No. I guess my husband didn't know how to do it or something." It was wonderful, and I loved every minute of it! He stayed the next day and about two weeks later I asked him if he was going to stay with me forever and ever. He just looked at me and said, "Give me a month and I will know more if I want to totally be with you." In another week he knew.

William and I and Paul all went to Paul's trailer to clean out his stuff so he could move in with me. William had a huge truck with a big wooden body on it that was almost heavier than the truck itself. You could hardly see the road over the hood while you were driving. It was dark and foggy that night. I was supposed to be the leader of the convoy, so that William could follow by the taillights of my Oldsmobile. But he was talking and getting to know Paul, and he missed a corner and went right out into the field. Paul said in a calm voice, "William, you're out in the field." William swerved back onto the road and tried to keep up with me. He was blowing his horn at me and getting all excited. Apparently, I was going too fast in the fog. So I stopped and let him be the leader. Then, he went so slowly in the fog that we didn't get home until late that evening. We went directly to bed, instead of unloading the load that was on the truck that night. William stayed upstairs.

We all had a good breakfast and started unloading the truck. I was so excited Paul was going to be my man. And no one or nothing is going to get in the way of that.

Chapter 35
Rachel

William came home one day and told me about this girl he had been seeing - I will call her Rachel. He wanted me to meet her family. William was very serious about this girl, and he wanted to marry her. He had an engagement ring ready to give her. At the time, her parents seemed to be nice people. William told me he had been there many times playing cards with them by candlelight, because they didn't have electricity, or running water or sewer service.

I couldn't believe my eyes when I walked into their trailer - they were so poor! They were poorer than I had been for a very long time. The family was a large family, and these days it is hard to raise a large family on a small income. William was so excited about my going there to meet his future wife's family. When I got home we had a conversation. He brought up the fact that Rachel had several brothers and sisters. "Does that mean that Rachel is fertile and I could give you

138

grandchildren?" "I believe so," was my answer. "She's kind of young, though. William. You should wait a couple of years till Rachel is old enough to care for a baby properly." But he said, "I have been saving baby clothes already, Mom."

I was really excited for him that he had found someone special, too. A few weeks went by and William called me on the phone to tell me Rachel was there in his house and Rachael wanted to have sex. I said, "William you should wait a little while. How old is Rachel?" "In two weeks Rachel will be 16 years old. And I am 19 years old. I know there is an age difference. But it never bothered you and Dad, Mom." My reply was, that was a different story all together. I then asked, "William, how did Rachel get to your house?" "She ran away from home to be with me. Rachel loves me, mom! Everyone else is telling me to go for it. You're the only one telling me to wait." I didn't know what to say.

William and Rachel went ahead. A few days later, William called me from jail. He told me that they wouldn't let him out of jail until he signed this document stating he was a pedophile. I should have acted on this immediately. They held my son in there for 4 months in jail. And they still wouldn't let him out until he finally signed the stupid paper. I should have gotten a lawyer and fought it, because it was consensual sex.

The girl's mother had pressed charges against my son, because her daughter had run away from home to be with my son. She didn't go home after William was jailed, either. That tells me she really loved my son and wanted to be with him.

My son was put onto the Maine Sex Offender Registry with all of the hard-core sex offenders. It was consensual sex with his girlfriend.

That's when William's trouble started happening at his home, also. The town posted a picture of him at the town office for everyone to see and judge him, when they had no idea of what his crime really was. When you go to see what he had done on the Sex Offender Registry, they don't tell what he had really done to be on the registry. It lists the following: address, work place, eye color, hair color, height, weight, birth date, school, zip code, attendance, statutory citation, name of crime for which the registrant was convicted, and a photograph of the individual. The registry says nothing about what the crime was, or if it was consensual sex.

My son started to be picked on by the town and by some of his neighbor's kids. William had to be on his toes every single minute because he was constantly being harassed by people who didn't even know him, or what crime he had committed.

One day Paul and I went to visit William. There was

a young man out in the yard harassing my son. We jumped out of the car, and proceeded down the driveway. Paul got right in this little jerk's face, and said, "Is there a problem here?" The little jerk said, "Oh, no, not anymore," and left. We found out later that he had asked William's friend, "Who is that guy? And is he some kind of a giant or what?"

Even the code enforcement officer was bothering William about all of the cars he had in his driveway. He was a junk man, so what did he expect my son to have in his yard? I guess people call it a recycling engineer now. Everyday my son would go out searching for metal to take into the recycling shop in Bangor to make extra money, to buy a better place for him and his next girlfriend, because Rachel was out of the picture. So we went over one day to help William put up a building to hide some of the stuff he had lying around to try and please the code enforcement officer. But it didn't work.

William had to find another place to live and he was saving every penny he could to do this. He was looking at a piece of property of 100 acres in Charleston to make his own junkyard and he wanted to have lots of kids to help him in it. That was my son's dream.

William tried so hard to please so many people, and to do good things by them. One day, William came over to the house and started adjusting the wood stove's flue. The house filled up with smoke. Paul said to me, "Let's go, Shirley." We jumped into the car and away we went. I looked over my shoulder and saw William throw his hands into the air. We were gone a few hours and when we came home everything was fine again.

Chapter 36

Dexter, Maine

When Paul moved into my house he brought his Rottweiler named Rotti. It was an American breed, much larger than a German Blockhead. Paul had told me that if I left him there alone in my trailer, he would just jump right through a closed window to be with me. I might as well take him with me, or there would be trouble from his being there alone. Paul brought his skidder chain with him and chained him to a telephone pole in the yard. I had never even seen a skidder chain before, and the sight of it was enough to tell me how strong this dog really was. Paul had gotten Rotti when he was 16 months old, and the dog must have been beaten a lot, because he didn't like to be corrected.

One day I made a lasagna and banana bread. We decided to go somewhere and left the stuff on the stove. My dogs Trixie and Daisy never bothered it at all, but Rotti was a very smart dog. We had put him out in the mudroom while we were gone, so that he wasn't in the house. He lifted the little latch and walked right in. Rotti ate the rest of the lasagna and the entire banana bread, also. We were not very happy. Paul put him outside on his skidder chain in the yard for the rest of the day. We went out later, and he was gone. Someone had come up in our yard and took him off the chain. We searched the neighborhood, and found him down at our neighbor's house. "Oh, no, that's not your Rotti. We just got him the other day," was their reply. After a few hours, and driving up and down the road, he came back.

It was about 10:00 am and we had been up for a while. I made French toast. William loves my French toast, and he had come over to get some car parts up in the field that someone wanted. I was still in my bathrobe. Paul had taken Rotti out to do his business. My dogs went up in the field with William, so they were all set. I told William that French toast doesn't take very long to make, and to come right back or at least when I call you. He said, "Take care of Paul and I will be right down." So I proceeded to make brunch.

William walked into the living room and Rotti growled at him. William immediately left. But Rotti had taken a big crap right on my floor. Paul discovered it and started to correct Rotti. That's when all heck broke loose. What we didn't know was that Rotti had eaten an entire bag of bone meal that I was using on my flower bulbs. It caused a chemical reaction in his brain, making him aggressive, so Rotti went after Paul. He grabbed Paul and started chewing on Paul's left arm. I didn't know what to do. I had never seen anything like this happen before. All I could think of to do was try to distract Rotti's attention away from Paul. So I grabbed a piece of firewood and started hitting him. Rotti totally ignored me and continued to chew on Paul.

It was as if a nightmare just unfolded into our laps. Paul managed to pry Rotti's mouth off his left arm, and that's when Rotti went to his right arm. Paul hollered, "Shirley, you've got to do something now before he kills me." My brain started to realize this was a life or death situation. I went directly to my nightstand by the bed and got my 38 revolver. Paul had wrestled Rotti into the hall. The dog was still hanging from his right arm. I told Paul to step back and hold him away from his body. I put the gun right on Rotti's chest, and I shot him. Rotti just sat there and looked at me like, "That didn't hurt, what did you do that for?" I proceeded to put two more bullets into him just in case. That was the first time I had ever killed anything, but it had to be done, or the dog might have killed Paul. I loved Paul far too much to let that happen to him. It very well could have been William, as well. Rotti growled at him first.

I screamed out of the house for William to come

down now. He knew by the tone of my voice that something had happened. When I think about it, I feel he was a little proud of me, though. I killed the dog all by myself and saved Paul. Meanwhile, Paul was running around the house with blood pulsating out of his wounds. "You've got to do something here, Shirley, or I am going to bleed to death." I tore off the tie on my robe and made a tourniquet. William said that we needed to get him to the hospital. I said I would call an ambulance. William said that it would take too long, and to just get in the car and he would drive. I was too shaken up to drive. So we all got into my Oldsmobile with the 350 rocket engine and away we went. Mayo Regional Hospital in Dover-Foxcroft was the closest hospital around, about 30 miles away. At one point, William was driving so wildly that Paul spoke up and said, "Slow down William, I don't want to die on the way to the hospital." He was blowing the horn and going 50 or more through town, but he got us there in one piece.

When we got there I said to the doctor, "I did the best I could by putting a tourniquet on it;" he said, "I wish you wouldn't have." I replied that I thought he would bleed to death, but he said no. It looked like a lot of blood to me coming out of his arms. The doctor stitched him up and we went home. Paul was in bed for about two weeks with this. It took the dogcatcher four

146

hours to come and get Rotti off of my kitchen floor.

There were a lot of chores to do alone while Paul recovered from his dog bites. I tried really hard to keep things going while Paul was laid up in bed. I carried wood and did my normal chores around the house. This was in late February; there was snow still on the ground. Paul and I had just gotten together a few weeks earlier. Then it happened to me. I was outside in those little flip-flops, carrying wood in the snow. I slid and carried that entire armful all the way to the ground. I broke my ankle so badly that I have a Titanium Plate and Canulatted screws in it today.

I was on the couch where Paul was just days ago, with a cast on my foot. I had broken both of my feet previously. So here I was with nothing to do but knit. I made an afghan for my niece in the 6 weeks on the couch. Paul made me stay there and rest. He wasn't my husband who made me get up and do everything after a week, including walking the dog with a cast on my foot. Paul was and still is a very wonderful caring man. Just the opposite of my husband, a self-centered egotist from the get go.

I know I'm supposed to forgive and forget, but there's one thing I am having an awful time trying to forgive my husband for making me do. He made me quit my job at Eastern Maine Medical Center in Central Sterile Supply. I loved cleaning and sterilizing the instruments for the operating room. I actually had an important job at last. In some small way I was actually helping people, instead of cleaning toilets for the rest of my life. I can forgive my husband for so many other cruel things he did to me, but that job just made me feel so good about myself! I should have just said go screw yourself period end of discussion I am going to work there whether you like it or not, and that's that. But I have changed a lot since then, and Paul has helped me to become who I am today. I owe him a lot for all he has done for me in the last six years.

We went over to visit William at his trailer in Corinth and hopefully get a picture of all of us. At the last minute William grabbed an old mason jar that he dug up from an old dump up in Bangor, at a public dump that was closed in 1910.

He dug up nothing but the bottles, jugs, metal, and an occasional pig bone. William loved going there growing up. No other kid in school had that to say at share time in first or second grade, and he did. We all did bring home a pretty good bottle now and then - a poison bottle or even something rare once in a while.

When William was a boy, there was one place I truly loved in the old farmhouse. At the top of the stairs was a huge coat closet. I made it into my very own workshop, and my husband could see me, so he didn't need to holler, "Where are you, I can't see you." It was a place I could go to get away from the hollering and bickering. Like William, he spent most of his time in his room. William did it to avoid fighting with his father. One day, I was outside mowing the lawn, and the mower ran out of gas. My husband came out and said, "Where are you, I can't see you." I hollered back, "It ran out of gas." I had to fill it up. My husband was in the house watching television and smoking dope. I did enjoy mowing though, it kept me physically fit. But, at the same time, it made me feel like some kind of kid when he hollered at me.

Paul never hollers at me or forces me to work. And what a relief it is to go into MacDonald's bathroom and not have my husband or William at the door when I come out. If my husband didn't want to stand by the restroom door, he made William stand at the door. I felt foolish when I would come out and see people looking at me, like I was some kind of an idiot that couldn't go to the bathroom by myself.

My sister and mother called me one day and told me how much William looked like Leonardo Dicaprio. I agree. Only his height is a little different.

Chapter 36
Hartland, Maine

Fall was about to be here and Paul was getting itchy feet and wanted to move into his own place. He said to me, "If you're going to be my woman, we need to get out of this house and find something of our own to live in." But I was left with a house full of furniture and everything you could imagine. We needed money to get something of our own anyway, so I called up a local auctioneer. He came over and helped me pack stuff up and move it to the auction to be sold. I was able to put some money down on a piece of property and buy an older mobile home. We bought 57 acres in Hartland, Maine. I put in a well and septic. Paul did all of the rest of the things as far as the plumbing, electric, and he hooked up the sewer and even put the plywood skirting on. So we had a new place to live, although we had to wait 6 weeks to have the power hooked up. The trailer was 350 feet from the road, and the power company had to cut down some trees.

Shirley Turner

The first spring there was rainy. And we had a 14 x 70 foot flood in front of our steps to the end of our trailer. We did complain to the people we bought the land from. They said, "Too bad if you don't like it, move." Come to find out years later that these same people had stolen four million dollars from poor people like me, by buying a piece of property and selling it to several different people, a true con game. They stole what little bit of money I had to invest. The man now is serving time in prison for embezzling money from many people here in Maine.

William saw the flood one day and couldn't believe his eyes. But the following year we got an excavator and Paul dug a trench all the way around the trailer. We didn't have a drop of water in front of our trailer after that. He did a lot around there that day with the machine. He dug out ditches that hadn't been dug for years and then put in a couple of postholes so we could put up a gate. Boy did the neighbors hate that! Paul even got an old plow truck the third year we were there, to keep the driveway clean after a snowstorm. Sometimes it seemed like he could hardly wait for another snowstorm to get out there and plow his own driveway. And the neighbors had to hire someone to do theirs. They were so jealous.

We did so much to that land, like plant flowers, fruit trees, and blueberry bushes. We cut down a lot of brush to make more places to plant other things. We improved it all together. Then we found out that we were never going to own it. That's when I stopped improving someone else's land for them. I did have some chickens and even a turkey that William came over to see. He picked it up, and said me, "Mom, this would make a fine Thanksgiving meal." I said, "William, it's a pet." I didn't have it long. I just didn't have the room for a turkey; they take a lot of room. Not like chickens, which can live in a rather small space.

The first year there we had only one television station all winter. The following year we got an antenna. We received four stations. Wow, we were living it up then! I did have some birds in the house to take care of and give me something to do also. That and every spring and fall I would get baby birds to sell. They are so special, especially to young children, to see them hatch and grow. This is something every child should experience. We had some struggles the first winter there. We got stuck in the ice and snow. The people we had bought this land from were supposed to dig a ditch around our trailer to keep the water from running under our trailer, but they truly didn't do much landscaping. We put several more loads of gravel into the back yard to build it up enough to avoid water from collecting underneath our trailer, after we saw what it had done the first year. This also rotted out the floors in our trailer. We remedied it for the coming spring.

The following year I went down to the town office and they told me I didn't own 57 acres, only 42 acres, and that someone else owned the other 13 acres of my land. I was suspicious of the whole situation. Then we had a visitor come to our door and state that he owned our mortgage. When I knew nothing at all about this. So I decided to do some investigating on my own, and discovered that there were two other people on my mortgage other than myself. The people who sold me my land had sold it before me and then after me. It didn't belong to me at all, and I had put so much sweat into this land.

But we stayed there for a few more years and dealt with a lot more problems to our trailer. There was one positive thing about living there. William could come over any time he wanted to.

Chapter 37
Hartland, Maine

My son called me from jail and told me that he was put in there for failure to register as a sex offender. He missed the appointment and they put him in jail for it. He told me that a friend was taking care of his birds and dog, so not to worry, and that he would be out of there in a few weeks. He was so happy to get out of there! I can't blame him a bit. He was behind bars and had no freedom.

When he got out, we went to the stock car races and out to eat at least once a week. We even went to the monster truck show they have here almost every year, or had a cookout in our backyard. William had steak over a wood fire for the first time. He couldn't believe how good it tasted. And Paul gave him the extra meat, which is something his father never would have done. He always had the extra one out of four steaks. Afterward, William asked me if I had any extra canned goods. I said, "Sure. You're getting awful skinny." He said, "Mom, they're not for me. There is a family that I know, that the kids are even skinnier than I was growing up. And I'd like to give these to them if it's all right with you." I said, "William, you're skinny." He said, "Please let me give these to them." I said okay. He said, "It's okay. I will eat chicken, bologna, and hotdogs - it doesn't matter." And he tooted his horn on the way down my 350-foot driveway, "Beep Beep I Love You Mom!" he would holler as he drove down the driveway.

The following fall I bought 300 daffodils to plant along the driveway, for spring's enjoyment. I thought that William might pick me a bouquet for Mother's Day, or any day that he was over to see Paul and me. It was a good half an hour drive from his house so I tried to be there when he was coming over, so I didn't miss him.

One day I saw him out during spring clean up. We were so glad to see each other, it had been awhile. He was always out picking metal to make money and hauling it to the recycling places. Every day, even when he was sick. He had to make the money to get another place to live rather than on the main street that he was on, because so many people were complaining to the town about his cars and stuff in his yard. It was only metal, but it was a mess to some people. He had a gold mine sitting right there in his yard. The price of metal had gone up in price so much at that time. There wasn't any real garbage to attract rats or anything like that in his yard.

A few days later he called me and told me about a girl that he had been seeing for a few weeks that he had met from the internet. He'd go all the way to Bath, Maine, to see her. He told me she was a very smart and pretty girl, who worked in the hospital. After a month went by he told me that she was pregnant. But it was another man's child, so they broke up and she was going to tell the other man.

My son was different from other people his age. He didn't drink, do drugs or even smoke cigarettes. He really didn't fit into the crowd, but he made the best of it when he was around others. A girl next door did come over to visit William sometimes. She even helped him clean his trailer a few times, just to help him out. She was a very nice girl, and I was hoping it would work out and she might move in permanently. But then my son found a girl on the internet. He told me she was a few years older than he. "Maturity is a good thing, William." was my reply. "And if you are compatible and get along, what's wrong with that." She cooked and cleaned William's trailer up, so you can't beat that. He was finally getting meals regularly and putting on some weight. That's all that really matters.

One evening we went over to see him, and he said,"I need to talk to you alone for a minute, Mom. She won't help me to do junk, though." I explained to him that she was a girl and most girls just don't do that. "But you did, Mom." "Well, I'm a little different from most girls." "You'd even go out and help Dad with any work he had to do on the car." "I know, William, but most girls are not raised the same way I was. They go to the beauty parlor and get their nails done regularly, they are prim and proper and don't like to get dirty. What can I say - I'm weird I guess. I don't mind getting a little dirty or greasy. It washes off easy."

Chapter 38
Ex-husband's Return

My ex-husband got out of prison shortly after that. He was living in a shelter. So William decided to take him in. He could live with William's new girlfriend and him. He wanted to get him off of the streets of Bangor, which was an honorable thing for William to do. But I didn't think the girlfriend liked it very much. They told me that my ex-husband didn't buy any groceries and complained about having so much chicken in prison. Boy that just added fuel to the fire, so they had chicken every other night on purpose. They were trying to get my ex-husband to either buy some food for the house or to move out. A few months of my ex-husband is enough to drive anyone up the wall!

William told me that he had to put a lock on the inside and the outside of his bedroom door. My ex-husband was either walking into their room when they were having sex or snooping when they were away from the house. He didn't help around the house either, not even to bring in the wood for the stove, to keep warm. So William was under a lot of stress at this time of his life.

They were so glad when my ex-husband found a place to live, and finally moved out. Oh, their own place again to do whatever they wanted! But while he was there he discovered that I was at the auction a lot. He had to go and see me there. William told me that I said it was okay for him to tell him, but I don't remember that. Why would I say that when I had a protection from abuse order on him to begin with? It just didn't make sense. But he came there, and after the auction, I called and reported it. They told me I should have done it while the auction was on, to catch him in the act. So he got away with not going back to prison, because he was on probation, and several times after that also. He finally spent 15 days in jail for violating the order. My son was very angry with me. When I called him even a month later he hung up on me. And that was the last time I heard his voice.

Chapter 39
Stephen Marshall

On Easter Sunday of 2006, April 16th, I awoke up like I had a terrible dream. I was sweating, and sat right up in bed. I was upset over something, and didn't know what it was. I went about my day. Doing things around the house, before I set out to do my little cleaning job I had. I stopped at the local store and bought a salad for supper. It must have been about 4:30 pm when I got to my work place. I did some things there, and then my cell phone rang. Paul was on the other end. He told me to come home and made me promise to be careful driving home. "I have some bad news for you," he said. "Your son was murdered today. I just heard it on the 6:00 news. And another man from Milo named Joseph Gray also." I said, "No it couldn't be, you must have misunderstood. It can't be my son." He said, "Come home now. And remember to be careful - you promised."

All the way home, I kept saying, "It must be someone else. It couldn't be my only child." I immediately called the state police and asked them. They said yes. I asked why someone didn't call me, the officer didn't know. But I'm sure that they must have asked my ex-husband to contact me. When the 11:00 pm news came on, I still didn't believe it. That's when the whole story started to unravel. I couldn't eat sleep, or anything for three days. All I could do is cry. On the third day, I went over to my son's house. It had started sinking in that I would never get to see my only child William again on this earth.

My husband was there already, cleaning out my son's possessions. I couldn't believe it. Then my husband put a protection order on me! He had abused me for the last 22 years of my life with him. The judge saw right through that and threw it out of court.

I started hearing more about the killer all the time on the television news and in the newspaper. This 20-year-old young man, who was a dishwasher at a Chinese restaurant, was from Canada. He had killed my only child, William. His name was Stephen Marshall. On April 13th, 2006, he had come from Cape Breton, Nova Scotia, with a backpack, computer and a knife. He planned to visit with his father, who lived in Houlton, Maine, and was having health problems. It was the first time he had seen his father since they lived in Idaho many years earlier. Stephen stayed at his father's house. On April 15th, on Saturday evening,

The Destroying Angel

Stephen asked his father if they could go to the firing range to do a little practice shooting on Easter Sunday, but bad weather kept them from going. "We will go when the weather clears up, son," was his father's reply. But Stephen couldn't wait that long.

Saturday night, after his father had checked on him for bed, Stephen gathered up his computer and backpack and knife and stole three of his father's guns, an ak47 assault rifle, a 22 handgun and a colt 45 handgun. He got his father's keys and stole his white Toyota pickup because on his way from Canada he had car trouble and didn't have his own vehicle. He had to take his father's truck to do his crime.

He was supposed to go to work on Saturday, washing dishes at the Chinese restaurant in Cape Breton. He didn't call or show up. He had spent two days cleaning and oiling up his father's guns. He had his mind set to kill some unsuspecting victims. He headed south with 34 names and addresses and even their places of employment of sex offenders throughout Maine. He arrived in Milo, Maine at 3:15 am, and shot his first victim, Mr. Joseph Gray. He had been sleeping on his couch when his 5 dogs started barking as they always did when something was outside that wasn't supposed to be there. His wife got up and saw a shadow outside the window. She saw a man in a dark colored jacket. He shot Joseph Gray four times in the torso and once in his mouth. His wife was stunned over the sudden loss of her husband. She herself narrowly was missed by one of the seven bullets that were fired. The police found several Canadian cigarette butts at the scene. The murderer had been standing there for quite some time, stalking Mr. and Mrs. Gray.

Stephen Marshall never blinked an eye. He just got into his father's truck and got on the road again. The police got there and started their investigation. The killer was still out there. Stephen Marshall stopped his vehicle at several other sex offenders' houses and knocked at four other doors on his way to Corinth, Maine. It was about 11 miles from his last murder. No one came to their doors. It was very early in the morning still.

He drove another 10 miles to Corinth. He knocked on my son's trailer door at about 6:30 am. William didn't go to the door then. Stephen Marshall left and came back about 8:15 am and knocked again. My son had a policy that when someone knocked at his door, he always went to his rear trailer door to see the car at the top of the road. Stephen Marshall was very smart; he had parked his car on the other side of the road, so that it wasn't visible from my son's rear door. So William ran back to the bedroom to get his sweat pants on, because he had been in bed, with his girlfriend. He then went to the door. Stephen Marshall was on the other side of William's front door, with the Colt 45 pistol aimed at the door. My son swung the door open, like he always did to welcome someone to his home.

Stephen Marshall started firing into William's body. I know that my son struggled with the gun and Stephen Marshall on the other end, because there was a shot in my son's foot, and in his arm, where he put it up to his face to protect it. That's when Stephen Marshall shot my son in his mouth. Stephen Marshall emptied the Colt 45 into my son's body. There was a bullet in his torso and three bullets in his chest, one through his left hand that went into his mouth that took out all of his teeth on one side. I know my son fought for his life that day. He wouldn't have gone down easy - he was very strong and healthy -he was 6 feet tall and 215 lbs and only 24 years old. But the bullets still took him to the floor of his trailer. He lay there gurgling in his own blood while Stephen Marshall stood over him, watching him die. My son called out to his girlfriend, "Honey, come help me." She ran to the door and there was Stephen Marshall standing looking at my son William.

She had been in bed and was barefoot. She ran out the door after Stephen Marshall. She ran up to the top of the road and watched Stephen Marshall get into his father's white Toyota pickup truck. Stephen Marshall was still gawking at her. He did a U-turn in the middle of the road. He came over to her side of the road and made a motion with his hand like he was going to kill her as well. She managed to get his license plate number. She kept saying the license plate number in between screams for help. She ran to the neighbor's house for help. But when she returned my son was dead.

Stephen Marshall had murdered two sex offenders and was on the road again. He was driving as fast as he could to get away from the scene. The police were all coming down the road towards him. While he was trying to make his escape on Route 15 in Corinth, he stopped at a farmer's market to get directions to Bangor, Maine. He was on his way to the bus station in Bangor.

He hung around the bus terminal. After leaving his father's Toyota pickup at the Sawyer Ice Arena in Bangor, he boarded a Vermont Transit bus line going south to Boston at 1:45 pm. Still armed and dangerous. He had names of sex offenders in Vermont and New Hampshire. But he decided to go to Boston authorities believe, hoping to kill some more sex offenders in the Boston area before he got caught for his crime. He left some clues behind: in the bathroom were several bullet casings he had left for police to discover.

He arrived at South Station in Boston at 7:30 pm.

The Destroying Angel

The police surrounded the bus. The bus driver was instructed to put on the overhead lights. Stephen Marshall was 13 seats behind the bus driver. He took the Colt 45 from his backpack and held it under his chin to kill himself. When he pulled the trigger, brain matter spattered all over 5 passengers. Stephen Marshall was declared dead later at the Boston Medical Center at 11:25 pm.

The state of Maine sex offender registry was taken off line for 24 hours, with 2,200 registered sex offenders on it at the time. Some people said that Stephen Marshall was a lighthearted young man that liked Cherry Coke, loud music, and had never even gotten a parking ticket in his life. But he had a lot of hatred for gays, drag queens, and didn't care for human diversity apparently. Anyone who was a little different from him was on his bad list. His idea of distinguishing who was a sex offender was the way he or she smiled. He created his own website in the panhandle in Idaho. On his web site, in between spaces, he had pictures of small cute disemboweled animals he had tortured and killed. He also believed in getting himself a Russian mail order bride someday. At the bottom of his website page, he wrote, *For the love of lesbian space monkeys just click the damn button please*. He had an image of Jesus armed with an assault rifle knocking on a door on his web site. He also told a friend that pedophiles were the scum of the earth.

I just wish that he would have stopped and asked my son about fixing his vehicle, instead of killing my son. William probably would have driven all the way to Houlton, fixed his car for him, and only asked for his gas money, even if it would have taken all day. He would have been doing something good for someone that day, and that's all that would have mattered to my son. William was a wonderful young man that certainly didn't deserve to die. But Stephen Marshall took the light of my life away from me. I wish he could have known my son. How good and kind he was to everyone! Everyone I ever came in contact with said what manners my son had and how he loved life. He cared for and loved for so many people in his life! Later, someone wrote on the internet that her car had broken down on Route 15 in Kenduskeag. A hundred cars must have gone by her. My son William was the only one that stopped to help her get her car going again.

Stephen Marshall missed out on so much, not getting to know my son. I just wish he had tried to, rather than kill him like he did.

The police discovered that Stephen Marshall was born in Texas, moved to Nova Scotia, and then to Idaho after the divorce of his parents. He finished high school in Idaho, and moved to Nova Scotia with his mother and stepfather, who own a bed and breakfast.

Police were investigating whether Stephen Marshall was molested by a notorious pedophile that lived in the same town in Idaho. This man is serving a sentence of 30 years in prison for committing a crime against a 16-year-old boy. He is now 71 years old and still in prison. I do know that both men were shot in the mouth and I suspect that Stephen Marshall may have been forced to perform oral sex on someone himself, which may have driven him to this crime. I feel very sad for Steven Marshall's family, because they lost a loved one as well.

After Stephen Marshall had killed himself on the bus, the bus driver was depressed and may have felt guilty for not checking passengers with his hand-held metal detector. He killed himself six months later on the Cooks Corner Road in Brunswick, Maine. But he shouldn't have. He didn't commit the crimes. He was a man from Bowdoinham, Maine. He was a soft-spoken, gentle soul, who really loved people and enjoyed his job. He was helping other people, just like my son William did every day of his life. The bus driver was found in November at 10:20 in his van in the junkyard with a lengthy note. He died apparently from asphyxiation.

The State of Maine Sex Offender Registry Law was passed in 1996. There are 2700 registered offenders in the State of Maine. There are 500,000 registered sex offenders nationwide. Mrs Gray did an interview later about Stephen Marshall, and called him Monster Marshall. All of this might have been prevented. In 2001, Marshall was arrested and charged with threatening with an assault rifle while standing in his doorway. He was attempting to break up a fight among some young men in his yard. Stephen Marshall must have slipped through the cracks. He received no counseling, no probation, nothing. He received a slap on the wrist and the police let him go. You would think that particular incident would have sent some kind of warning sign to someone before all of this happened.

My son William's slogan was *Where there's a Will there's a way*; everyone called him Will. At night we would say, "Good night, see you in the morning," just like the Walton's did every night on that show. I know that Stephen Marshall was supposed to be an outstanding citizen in his community and a church going person. I don't and probably never will understand why he just went off the handle and went on a vigilante rampage. Why did he have such a terrible hatred towards different people with different ideas in life? God made people different because it would be such a boring terrible place if we were all the same.

But I have my memories of my son. Stephen Marshall can't take them away from me. I just wish that my son had been able to bury me, instead of me having to bury my only child. There were 250 people at Stephen Marshall's funeral, the killer. But at my son's funeral, there were 30 - 40 people, the victim. The State of Maine is considering putting a tier system in place for the sex offender registry, now that my son is gone. So perhaps my son's life didn't go in vain. He may have saved many lives today by dying at Stephen Marshall's hands. They are even considering taking low-level offenders off the registry entirely, for offenders such as my son. He only received a misdemeanor for his crime, and someone today that has consensual sex with a minor, like my son did, won't be on the computer, only at the police station. I never looked at the registry until the loss of my son.

They are supposed to change the law in 2009. There are 3,134 Registered Sex offenders in Maine today, and 89 unregistered sex offenders. There are 3 different classifications. You can find all of this information online on your computer under title 34 AMRSA, chapter 15. The law was put into effect in 1999. The public has a lot of personal information on the sex offender, as mentioned earlier. Any additional information about the registrant, for example, if the person was convicted of another crime, is available for a cost of $25.00. There is also a list at your local City Hall or Town Office. The information is updated daily. There is also a 24-hour hotline in place at this time.

Shirley Turner

Maybe his death will do some good for someone else. I know I will miss my son every day for the rest of my life. He brought me so much joy over the 24 years that I had him in my life. From the minute he was born, he was the joy of my life. The Lord's greatest gift. No purer soul on earth. I had him for 24 years. The best years of my life. Sometimes I can hardly wait to see him again in heaven, on the day that God takes me home.

Epilogue
Patten Maine

I lived in Hartland Maine for most of a year, and every time I drove down my driveway I'd remember William cutting trees, coming over for cookouts, or just spending time with his mom. It was there that I tried to heal from losing my son, but it wasn't working. It was also while living there that I was hit by a car while pushing a shopping cart and injured. Medical bills piled up and I had to sue the person who hit me. When the lawsuit was completed, I received a little bit of money for my injuries that allowed me to pay most of my doctor bills.

My trailer was in poor shape, the rugs were old and the electricity was gone on one side as a result of being flooded, because the owners never did the proper excavation work, and mold was growing in some of the rooms and making me sick.

The original owner contacted me to see if I would want to buy a couple of acres from him, but I had already paid $42,000 dollars for the trailer and forty-two acres.

I was so disgusted with the state of the trailer that I decided to sell it and try to buy a real house, but with my income being so low I could only get a loan for places in central Maine that weren't habitable, so I decided to do a little bit of online investigating, and found an old farmhouse that needed some work in Patten, Maine for 40,000 dollars. The downstairs had all been renovated, but the upstairs needed work. I could live downstairs and fix up the upstairs

I really wanted to leave Hartland, because I was constantly reminded of my son.

As much as I suffered from being molested, and from the beatings from my ex-husband, that wasn't a quarter of the trauma I felt from losing my son. He was my entire life for his twenty-four years. We knew each other's thought and feelings before we even said them. When he was murdered I lost almost everything. If Paul had not been at my side, I would have lost my sanity, and likely wouldn't be here today. The love we have for each other made me strong and helped me to cope with my son's death.

So the house in Patten was 125 miles from Hartland and it took us four or five trips in our pick up truck and trailer to get both of our belongings and William's.

I wish I could say that all has been better since we moved, but it hasn't been that way at all. We should have done better research on the property we bought, as we have been embroiled with the sellers in a dispute, which has made me terrified of them at times.

After moving to Patten, at the suggestion of former State Legislator Bill Diamond, I began attending hearings and meetings in Augusta, regarding changing the way Maine's Sex Offender Registry is organized and about who should or should not be on it. Senator Diamond told me he was writing a book—since published as The Evil and the Innocent—that would discuss the dire need to improve protection of children from predators and to ensure that such people are not allowed to reoffend. He also argues for a tiered system for the registry, which differentiates between people like my son who are guilty of minor consensual transgressions and those who rape and otherwise abuse innocent children. His work has meant so much to me, and though Augusta is 200 miles from Patten, Paul and I tried to be there every time Senator Diamond thought it was important.

Bill Diamond is a very fine man who cares deeply for all Mainers, especially the most vulnerable. It was often difficult to attend these meetings, as I was the only parent there who'd lost a child in the way I lost William.

If nothing else comes from this book, I hope that the public will come to see how serious the issue of child abuse and rape is, and that a one-size-fits all Registry is not only counter productive, but potentially lethal. When his book came out, Senator Diamond sent me a signed copy that I cherish.

Then my sister called me and told me that my ex-husband was in the Togus Veterans Hospital near Augusta, and was dying from lung and brain cancer. She added that if I was to see him before he died I needed to do so right away. For reasons I cannot fully understand, I went. He was weak and frail, having lost a great deal of weight. He cried the entire time I was there, and gave me three hundred dollars he said was for gas. I wondered if it was the only way he could say he was sorry for what he had done to me, or if he was crying for himself.

He was transferred to a rehabilitation center in Brewer and I visited him there. I walked into the lobby to find my mother sitting there talking to a woman I didn't know. She didn't even acknowledge me. I asked her if she knew who I was, and all she said was, "Yes, I know who you are," and went back talking to the other woman. To this day when my mother talks to others she refers to me only as, "That thing from Maine."

I continued to my ex-husband's room, where I found my sister, niece, nephews, and my sister's boyfriend. It was great to see my family, and to stay overnight in my sister's cottage, where she made a spaghetti feed for all of us.

The following day Paul and I went to see my ex-husband, and he gave Paul a hand-written letter with permission to clean out his trailer. After every trip into Brewer to see him, we'd take the long way home and collect things from the trailer. (He kept a key hidden underneath a bible on a stand next to the door.) There was a dumpster on site and we put many things into that. His social worker noted that it was odd for someone with a veteran's pension to have so few valuable possessions.

I suspect he spent most of his money on marijuana, which may have contributed to his lung cancer—I can only guess at that.

After a very short stay in Brewer, my ex-husband passed away at the age of 68.

When I told my therapist that my sister wanted me to attend his funeral she thought it better not to do so. She said I'd cried over years of abuse and didn't need to cry for him at his funeral. I thought about how until he was in the hospital I hadn't seen any family in almost ten years. Then my nephews were little boys and my niece a young girl who now was grown up and working.

Paul has become a grandfather and, as a result, I am a grandmother and there is great joy in that. Perhaps because I have known so much sorrow, I take heart in the joy of family. Paul and I do everything together, and I never thought I could meet such a wonderful man. I diligently attend counseling, but suffer from PTSD and sometimes he hardly gets a break from me in his face, but somehow it works and we hardly ever fight or even disagree. I am truly blessed.

Paul, too, has endured much loss and sadness since we moved to Patten. His brother Danny was killed riding a three-wheeled ATV, and his wife was so devastated that she committed suicide a year later. Eighteen months later, and a year after losing her legs to diabetes, Paul's mother died. He has been resolute and strong through all of this. He has given me much to be thankful for.

Still, not a day goes by that I don't think of William and wish he were here with me.

I want to thank Bruce Pratt for believing in my book project when so many others did not. He never gave up and encouraged me when I had given up on myself. We could not have done this without the wonderful Tina Passman who donated her time and talents to get the manuscript into the proper format, and made sure this was always my story in my voice. She is an angel.

CPSIA information can be obtained
at www.ICGtesting.com
Printed in the USA
JSHW081922210323
39261JS00001B/18

9 781944 393632